I0024343

Richard Le Gallienne, Arthur Henry Hallam

The Poems of Arthur Henry Hallam

Together with an essay on the lyrical poems of Alfred Tennyson; edited with an

introd. by Richard Le Gallienne

Richard Le Gallienne, Arthur Henry Hallam

The Poems of Arthur Henry Hallam
Together with an essay on the lyrical poems of Alfred Tennyson; edited with an introd. by Richard Le Gallienne

ISBN/EAN: 9783744767552

Printed in Europe, USA, Canada, Australia, Japan

Cover: Foto ©Thomas Meinert / pixelio.de

THE POEMS OF

ARTHUR HENRY HALLAM

TOGETHER WITH HIS ESSAY
ON THE LYRICAL POEMS OF
ALFRED TENNYSON

EDITED WITH AN INTRODUCTION
BY RICHARD LE GALLIENNE

LONDON : ELKIN
MATHEWS & JOHN
LANE, VIGO ST.

NEW YORK : MAC-
MILLAN & COMPY
MDCCCXCIII

CONTENTS

CONTENTS

CONTENTS

CONTENTS

NOTE

THERE have been two editions of Hallam's 'Remains' previous to the present one. The following are the collations of each :—

(1) Remains, | in Verse and Prose, | of Arthur Henry Hallam. | *Vattene in pace, alma beata e bella.* | Ariosto. | Printed by W. Nicol, 51, Pall Mall. | MDCCCXXXIV. | pp. xl, 363.

This, printed for private circulation, contains a prefatory memoir by the poet's father.

(2) Remains in Verse and Prose | of | Arthur Henry Hallam. | With a Preface and Memoir | *Vattene in pace, alma beata e bella.* | Ariosto. | With Portrait. | London : | John Murray, Albemarle Street. | 1862. | pp. lx, 305.

In addition to the Memoir of Arthur Hallam, the prefatory matter also included a memoir of Henry Fitzmaurice Hallam, signed 'H. S. M.' and 'F. L.' (Henry Sumner Maine, and Franklin Lushington), and an 'advertisement' by the editor, as before, the poet's father. In this edition a few of the poems given in the first are not reprinted.

The present reprint, save in the correction of actual errors, follows the first edition.

The editor and publishers desire to express their acknowledgments to Mr. John Murray for his courtesy in a copyright difficulty of some delicacy ; as also to Mr. Maggs, the bookseller, for his kindness in lending them a copy of the very rare first edition for their purpose.

INTRODUCTION

The following first-fruits of a singularly promising young life are not, of course, recalled here as achievement in any way commensurate with, though sufficiently indicative of, the high powers of Arthur Hallam. Though they have, indeed, real literary value, it is not, perhaps, mainly for that that we cherish them, but rather for the means they afford us of realising the writer's beautiful personality. His friend has told us that

> 'The world which credits what is done
> Is blind to all that might have been.'

The world, indeed, must of necessity lay disproportionate stress on achievement, and all too little on character. It has less opportunity of seeing what a man is than what he does. Unless we be lifted up, we have little chance with the world. Hence the *éclât* which follows certain forms of greatness, and neglects others. The gift of friendship is in itself a greater thing than the gift of poetry in itself, but unless that friendship becomes dramatic it wears no earthly laurel. Arthur Hallam had both gifts: but whereas the one had scarcely time to bud, the other blossomed richly; for youth, though but the spring of poetry, is the very midsummer of friendship—

> 'The affinities have strongest part
> In youth, and draw men heart to heart.'

History blesses us with many legends of great friendships, but none more beautiful and moving than that of the friendship of Arthur Hallam and Alfred Tennyson. I write their names in the order the poet of their love would have them go, for there are many passages of *In Memoriam* which show that in their 'marriage of true minds' the poet regarded himself as the weaker vessel. His friend, not he, the 'master-bowman' who in those rapt circles of college talk 'would cleave the mark.' That this was no friendly exaggeration we have abundant testimony, and we have but to realise what it means to have a close friend of dominant intellect and magnetic personality in the most plastic period of our lives to conjecture how great an influence had Arthur Hallam on the development of Alfred Tennyson.

The son of the famous historian, Arthur Hallam had, of course, exceptional advantages for culture to start with. Still, the sons of eminent men are not invariably marked by precocity, and Arthur's precocity was certainly remarkable. He could not, indeed, like Sir John Suckling, speak Latin at the age of five, but in his father's memoir of him we are told that he could read it with 'tolerable facility' at the age of nine, and that at the age of seven 'he had already learned to read French with facility.' At the age of ten he had already written 'several tragedies, dramatic poetry being an early passion with him. Indeed, his precocity somewhat alarmed his father, by whom it was controlled rather than encouraged.

Born in 1811 (in Bedford Place, London), he had in 1818 spent some months with his parents in Germany and Switzerland, and had thus early been subjected to the broadening influences of travel. In 1820 he was sent to a preparatory school at Putney, and remained there two years. Then followed some months' further travel abroad, and in October 1822 he went to Eton, where he remained till 1827.

His father pronounces him at the end of his Eton period 'a good, though not perhaps a first-rate scholar, in the Greek and Latin languages,' and refers to his 'remarkable facility in mastering the modern languages.' The study of English literature, especially that of the old dramatists, had somewhat withdrawn him from classical studies. Fletcher was a favourite of his, but Shakespeare was his ruling passion. Among modern poets Byron was long one of his preferences, but later on he gave place to Wordsworth and Shelley. Of classical writers, says his father, 'he loved Æschylus and Sophocles (to Euripides he hardly did justice), Lucretius and Virgil; if he did not seem so much drawn to Homer as might at first be expected, this may probably be accounted for by his increasing taste for philosophical poetry.' Very soon in a debating society at Eton he gave evidence of the argumentative powers of his mind, and in 1827 his first poem, on a story connected with the Lake of Killarney, appeared in the *Eton Miscellany*. This poem, however, his father did not think well to reprint among his 'Remains.'

On leaving Eton in 1827 came an eight months' visit to Italy, the most formative experience of his life. Thus Dante and the other 'Tuscan poets' became a passion with him, and he speedily mastered Italian, with what success his own sonnets in that language may well be left to testify. Italian art too, as also German, had at this time a great influence upon him. One of the last days of his life was spent lingering among the Venetian pictures of the Imperial Gallery of Vienna.

In October 1828 he was entered at Trinity College, Cambridge, as the pupil of the Rev. William Whewell. Charles and Alfred Tennyson had also entered the same college in the same term, and soon the three became the centre of that 'band of youthful friends,' including such other men as Richard Monckton Milnes, R. C. Trench, F. D. Maurice, James Spedding, Henry Alford, and Charles Merivale. Hallam soon attained eminence in this little coterie of 'The Apostles,' as it called itself, and soon too had Tennyson and he struck up that deeper friendship, the memory of which was to re-echo through the whole of Tennyson's life and inspire his highest song.

Early in 1829 they competed together for the Chancellor's Prize Poem, the subject, as the reader well knows, being 'Timbuctoo.' The result is, of course, a commonplace of literary history. To Hallam's poem, doubly interesting in the connection of his friend's success, it will be necessary to refer again.

Next year (1830) we find the friends together at Somersby Rectory, planning a joint volume of poems, a project, however, nipped in the bud by Hallam's father. The latter also enjoined silence in another matter,—the attachment which during this Somersby visit had been ripening between Arthur and Tennyson's sister. As early as 'Jan. 1831,' we find Hallam, in one of the most beautiful of the poems that follow—that 'To the Loved One'—thus writing of their love:

'Even now begins that holy life,
For when I kneel in Christian prayer,
Thy name, my own, my promised wife,
Is blent with mine in fondest care.
Oh pray for me that both may know
That inward bridal's high delight,
And both beyond the grave may go
Together in the Father's sight.'

Hallam is probably referring here to a troth known only to themselves, for at the time of writing he was away from Somersby, and it was not till his next visit, later in the year, that a private engagement between him and Emily Tennyson became known in the family, an engagement to be kept secret till Arthur's majority, in deference to his father. In the summer of 1832, however, silence was no longer necessary. He was of age, had taken his degree and left Cambridge, and his next step was to be law at the Inner Temple. Meanwhile, he spent the summer weeks at Somersby, whence he wrote thus to his friend Trench : 'I am now at Somersby, not only as the friend of Alfred Tennyson, but as the lover of his sister. An attachment on my part of near two years' standing, and an engagement of one year's, are, I hope, only the commencement of an union which circumstances may not impair, and the grave itself not conclude.'

To return, however, to 1830 : the friends had also during that year made a wild visit to the Pyrenees. The war of Spanish Independence was to young men of that day what the fight for Italian Independence was to those born later. Hallam and Tennyson ardently watched the struggle, and even went so far as to actually play at conspiracy, carrying messages and money to certain of the insurgents. 'And a wild bustling time we had of it,' said Hallam. 'I played my part as conspirator in a small way, and made friends with two or three gallant men who have since been trying their luck with Valdes.' Mrs. Ritchie tells an amusing anecdote worth recalling in reference to this expedition. Tennyson, having crossed over from the Continent, was walking home through Wales. 'He went one day into a little wayside inn, where an old man sat by the fire, who looked up and asked many questions. "Are you from the army? Not from the army? Then where do you come from?" said the old man. "I am just come from the Pyrenees," said Alfred. "Ah, I knew there was a something," said the wise old man.'

Another still more important event in this year was the publication of *Poems, chiefly Lyrical.* Hallam's famous review of it in *The Englishman's Magazine* for August 1831 is reprinted in the present volume, and will be dealt with later on. In the same year, his last at Cambridge, he obtained the first College prize for English declamation, his subject being the conduct of the Independent party during the Civil War. This he followed up by an oration on the congenial theme of 'The Influence of Italian upon English Literature.' We see here in his choice of subjects the bent of his mind, his partiality for philosophical, literary, and historical studies, asserting itself. It was a bent which, together with his indifference to mathematics, made against his achieving great academical reputation. A somewhat defective memory was another drawback; but really such ambition was little to his taste, and more and more he was developing the more sympathetic gifts of poet and critic.

In October 1832 Arthur Hallam went up to London, working with a Mr. Walters, a conveyancer in Lincoln's Inn Fields, and living at 67 Wimpole St. 'You will always find me at sixes and sevens,' was, according to Mr. Waugh, his little joke upon his address. Earlier in the year he had written his vigorous criticism on Professor Rossetti's *Disquisizioni sullo Spirito Antipapale*, he had also cherished a design to translate the *Vita Nuova*, and had written memoirs of Petrarch, Voltaire, and Burke for 'the Gallery of Portraits;' but, for the time, literary studies were exchanged for some hard law reading—into which, according to his father, he entered 'not only with great acuteness but considerable interest'—with his favourite metaphysical researches for recreation.

Alas, there is little more to record. Arthur's health at Cambridge had given grave anxiety to his friends. 'A too rapid determination of blood towards the brain' was one of the alarming symptoms of an irregular circulation. But during his last year at Cambridge he had seemed stronger. However, an attack of intermittent fever, or influenza, during the spring of 1833, weakened him; and, travelling in Germany with his father during the autumn of the same year, a wet day brought on a return of the fever. But that, writes his father, was apparently subsiding, 'when a sudden rush of blood to the head put an instantaneous end to his life on the 15th of September 1833.' Sir Francis Doyle, in his *Reminiscences*, adds the touching detail that his father had been out for a walk through the streets of Vienna, and came back to find Arthur apparently asleep on the sofa. 'Mr. Hallam sat down to write his letters,' he continues, 'and it was only by slow and imperceptible degrees that a certain anxiety, in consequence of Arthur's stillness and silence, dawned upon his mind: he drew near to ascertain why he had not moved or spoken, and found that all was over.'

Medical examination proved that he could not, at the most, have lived for many more years. 'Those whose eyes must long be dim with tears,' writes the stricken father, 'and whose hopes on this side the tomb are broken down for ever, may cling, as well as they can, to the poor consolation of believing that a few more years would, in the usual chances of humanity, have severed the frail union of his graceful and manly form with the pure spirit that it enshrined.'

Arthur Hallam's remains were interred, as all lovers of English poetry know, in the chancel of Clevedon Church, in Somersetshire, on January 3, 1834.*

Many were the tributes from his friends (Mr. Gladstone and Monckton Milnes among others) to his high powers, thus suddenly laid waste, but fullest of all was their testimony to the manly beauty of his

* Mr. Jacobs, in his careful notes on *In Memoriam*, points out that the poet refers to his friend as being buried outside the church :

> 'I sing to him that rests below,
> And, since the grasses round me wave,
> I take the grasses of the grave,
> And make them pipes whereon to blow ;'

but surely it is hypercritical to insist on the literalness of a reference which one may well regard as made, and would expect to be made, in conventional poetic terms. Mr. Jacobs reads section LXVII. of the poem as though it referred merely to a tablet on the walls of Clevedon Church, but I cannot see how he contrives to limit the nature. 'Happily,' wrote one of them to Mr. Hallam, 'his reputation is not left to depend upon the scanty reminiscences of one or two youthful friends: the memorials which he has bequeathed to us of his mental powers, together with the unanimous consent of all who had an opportunity of knowing and appreciating him as he deserved, are amply sufficient to secure to him that to which he is entitled—the sincere and lasting regret of all good men that such a

---

passage to that meaning. The poet distinctly speaks of the church as Arthur's 'place of rest':

'When on my bed the moonlight falls,
I know that in thy place of rest
By that broad water of the west,
There comes a glory on the walls:

Thy marble bright in dark appears,
As slowly steals a silver flame
Along the letters of thy name,
And o'er the number of thy years.'

No one reading this without any previous knowledge could read it otherwise than as a reference to the poet's actual tomb. The disparity between it and the reference to the grass-grown grave obviously arises from the fact, that in the latter case the poet is making use of conventional imagery, and in the former is making use of actual detail.

mind should have been removed from among us at a time when the light of his matured genius, and the excellence of his moral nature, might have exercised so great and so beneficial an influence upon the happiness of mankind.'

In restricting the following selection from Hallam's writings to his poems and his Tennyson criticism, the intention has been the illustration of the more intimately personal qualities of his nature rather than that of his merely intellectual powers. These latter were very remarkable. The extent of his reading alone is astonishing in so young a man, but still more so is his mature employment of that reading, his philosophical breadth, his power of historical generalisation. It is inevitable that in his display of authorities one sometimes, so to say, smells the newness of a young man's learning. The older scholar is not so faultlessly *cap-à-pie*, his learning has lost its glitter in many a field. He moves with less clank of accoutrements. But, however that be, no one can deny that the young man's weapons were of the right temper, and that he used them with singular vigour and address.

His best essay is, I think, that on the elder Rossetti's *Disquisizioni sullo Spirito Antipapale.* The lofty judicial tone, never relaxed in the essays on Cicero and the Italian influence in English literature, occasionally gives way to a more familiar style. There is a twinkle in certain passages, the critic even banters the professor—the Ignatius Donnelly of Dante criticism. 'A man must be careful indeed,' he says, 'in whose words or actions Signor Rossetti would not discover something to help out his argument. If two persons at opposite ends of the world do but chance to light on the same mode of expression, our learned professor calls out, like honest Verges, "'Fore God, they are both of a tale!" For him there is mystery in the most trivial incident. He would think, with Sir Thomas Browne, "it was not for nothing David picked up *five* stones in the brook."' There is quite a Lamb-like turn about the last reference.

Dealing with Rossetti's cryptographic account of the *Vita Nuova*, his stately style grows finely impassioned. 'Certainly,' he says, 'until Signor Rossetti suggested the idea, we never dreamed of looking for Ghibelline enigmas in a narrative apparently so remote from politics. Nor did it occur to us to seek even for moral meanings, that might throw a forced and doubtful light on these obscurities. Whatever uncertain shape might, for a few moments, be assumed by the Beatrice of the *Commedia*, imparadised in overpowering effluences of light and music, and enjoying the immediate vision of the Most High, here at least, in the mild humility and modest nobleness of the living and the loving creature, to whom the sonnets and canzones are addressed, we did believe we were safe from allegory. Something indeed there was of vagueness and unreality in the picture we beheld: but it never disturbed our faith; for we believed it to arise from the reverential feeling which seemed to possess the poet's imagination, and led him to concentrate all his loftiest sentiments and pure ideas of perfection in the object of his youthful passion, consecrated long since and idealised to his heart, by the sanctities of the overshadowing tomb. It was a noble thing, we thought, to see the stern politician, the embittered exile, the man worn by the world's severest realities, who knew how sharp it was to mount another's stairs, and eat another's bread, in his old age; yet, amidst these sufferings and wounded feelings, recurring with undaunted memory to the days of his happy boyhood; not for purposes of vain regret; not for complaints of deceived expectation; not to colour the past time with the sombre tints of the present: but to honour human nature; to glorify disinterested affection; to celebrate that solemn, primeval, indissoluble alliance between the imagination and the heart.' There is somewhat too much of youthful declamation about the concluding sentences, but the passage remains, for all that, a moving piece of prose.

One striking feature of Hallam's criticism is his adherence to the first law of æsthetics—which, doubtless, his German reading had taught him—the law of Beauty. 'To every man, worthy the name of poet,' he instructs the singularly unpoetic father of a great poet, 'the first object is always the Beautiful.' No allegory, however wise and profound, can distract him from it. He may study such meanings as a diversion, a piece of by-play; but they never interfere with the grand purpose to which his 'spiritual agents are bent up.' They are limited then, not by speculations about the prospects of any party, Guelf or Ghibelline, but by the poet's own sense of harmonious fitness, that inward testimony, which affords to creative intellects a support during their work of thought, not very dissimilar from that which conscience supplies to all men in their work of life.'

Elsewhere he speaks of 'the worship of

Beauty' as 'a vocation of high and mysterious import, not to be relegated into the round of daily amusements, or confined by the superstitious canons of temporary opinion.'

Indeed, it seems to me that his great promise as a critic was in his union of two instincts that seldom go together, the æsthetic and historic. It was his rich endowment of the former that made him so sympathetic an interpreter of the poetic genius of his friend: for, if one poet more than another needs to be judged by the artistic temperament, it is Tennyson. Unfortunately, nothing is rarer among critics, who are able to apply every test, philosophic, ethic, historic, save the one which is alone to the purpose. Hence so much wrong-headed injustice done to Tennyson's reputation from time to time, and so much (artistically) mistaken exaltation of Browning.

It is really remarkable with what precision he, 'the master-bowman,' clove the mark in the essay on Tennyson, which the reader may study for himself in the present volume. His 'five distinctive excellences' make a singularly accurate and complete analysis of a genius which, it must be remembered too, he was only given to see in the bud. To these must be added the 'fairy fineness' of the poet's ear, and 'the strange earnestness in his worship of beauty.' Especially acute, and how prophetic of Tennyson's dramatic career, is his differentiation in speaking of the poet's 'power of embodying himself in ideal characters, or rather moods of character.' If Tennyson had but accepted that limitation of his dramatic talent, how much richer still would we have been, rich as we are in that lyric wealth which was his best gift. The essay has faults of immaturity: its introduction is a little top-heavy, and there is just a touch of that 'pomposity' about it at which Christopher North made his somewhat heavy-footed sallies. The young critic seems over-conscious that he is writing his first review, and feels it all the more necessary to assume occasional airs of experience. But, when all is said, it remains a singularly penetrative piece of criticism; interesting too as one of the early examples in England of that æsthetic criticism which is now so generally accepted amongst us.

In turning to Hallam's poetry, and remembering this æsthetic instinct of his, one is struck by the absence of the sensuous element, so marked in his friend's poetry. One feels at once that Wordsworth is *genius loci.* All is grave in tone, subdued in colour, reflective in mood. And of this influence the reader will notice several casual indications: the motto to *Timbuctoo*, the quotation towards the end of that poem from *Tintern Abbey*, the explicit reference in the sixth of the *Meditative Fragments*:

> 'I spake of Wordsworth, of that lofty mind,
> Enthronised in a little monarchy
> Of hills and waters . . .'

It was, we learn from this naively charming poem, one of the disappointments of friendship that a lady of his acquaintance could not see that poet with the same admiring eyes as he.

> 'It is a thing of trial to the heart,
> Of trial and of painful wonderment,
> To walk within a dear companion's voice,
> And hear him speak light words of one we hold
> In the same compass of undoubting love.'

Notice the beautiful phrase, 'within a dear companion's voice.'

The reader will also mark one or two respectful references to 'Mr. Coleridge': notably that in which he tells us that in the composition of a certain description in *Timbuctoo* 'my thoughts dwelt almost involuntarily on those few conversations which it is my delight to have held with that "good old man, most eloquent," Samuel Coleridge.' It will be interesting to recall the lines here:

> 'Methought I saw a face whose every line
> Wore the pale cast of Thought; a good, old man,
> Most eloquent, who spake of things divine.
> Around him youths were gathered, who did scan
> His countenance so grand and mild; and drank
> The sweet, sad tones of Wisdom, which outran
> The life-blood, coursing to the heart, and sank
> Inward from thought to thought. . . .'

Another characteristic picture, in these quaint lines from the poem on Melrose Abbey, is that of Sir Walter Scott with his dogs about him:

> 'It was a comfort, too, to see
>   Those dogs that from him ne'er would rove,
> And always eyed him rev'rently,
>   With glances of depending love.
> They know not of that eminence
> Which marks him to my reasoning sense:
> They know but that he is a man,
> And still to them is kind, and glads them all he can.'

The influence of Dante is less apparent than one would have expected, though the reader will have noticed it in the choice of metre for *Timbuctoo*, and be reminded of it in such lines as

> 'That winsome Lady sitting by my side,
> Whom still these eyes in every place desire.'

In regard to *Timbuctoo* one may agree with Arthur's father that 'notwithstanding its too great obscurity, the subject itself being hardly indicated, and the extreme hyperbolical importance which the author's brilliant fancy has attached to a nest of barbarians, no one can avoid admiring the grandeur of his conceptions, and the deep philosophy upon which he has built the scheme of his poem.' But the poem lacks at once that concreteness of description and that magic of fantasy so necessary for the treatment of such a dream: qualities startlingly present in the more successful poem of Hallam's friend—who, by the way, none the less attached an 'extreme hyperbolical importance . . . to a nest of barbarians,' his conception of his theme, indeed, being very similar to Hallam's.

I have noted two or three lines up and down the poems the build of which, perhaps fancifully, suggest Tennyson to one to-day:

> 'The garden trees are busy with the shower'—

and a description of noon-day wind dallying among the trees:

> 'Like an old playmate, whose soft welcomings
> Have less of ardour, because more of custom.'

But these are matters of mere incidental

interest. More pertinent is it to refer to the fine sonnets on Edinburgh—'Even thus, methinks, a city reared should be;' on Poetry; and those, now of such touching association, beginning, 'Lady, I bid thee to a sunny dome,' and 'Speed ye, warm hours.' All Hallam's sonnets are good—he was evidently one of the few poets born to the form. They remind me, in their blending of chaste reserve and tenderness, of the sonnets of William Caldwell Roscoe. The blank-verse fragments not only promise but mark the achievement of a considerable power over that difficult metre, which so many now-a-days think they can write, and so few can. They are particularly interesting to us from their references to friendship. There seems a sad fitness in the fact that the very first lines in the book should run:

> 'My bosom friend, 'tis long since we have looked
> Upon each other's face; and God may will
> It shall be longer, ere we meet again.'

Mrs. Ritchie's *Records* have made us familiar with a portion of that letter in verse, written out of a summer day in the garden, to 'Alfred':

> 'Alfred, I would that you beheld me now,
> Sitting beneath a mossy ivied wall
> On a quaint bench, which to that structure old
> Winds an accordant curve. Above my head
> Dilates immeasurable a wild of leaves.'

Indeed, few poetical 'remains' are so rich in such characteristic allusions as the gleaner loves to find. The books and places and hours he loved; his gentle, sensitive spirit; his high ideals: we gain intimate glimpses of all in these poems, often so beautiful for their own sake, and, happiest fortune of all, intimate glimpses of that 'lovely and pleasant' friendship which was the crowning sanctity of two noble lives. Alfred Tennyson was given years to build and beautify the immortal monument of their love. Arthur Hallam was given such a little time. But he has left his witness behind him, for all that, in the precious little sheaf of those poems that here make sweeter his sweet memory.

RICHARD LE GALLIENNE.

POEMS

A I

MEDITATIVE FRAGMENTS

IN BLANK VERSE

I

My bosom friend, 'tis long since we have looked
Upon each other's face; and God may will
It shall be longer, ere we meet again.
Awhile it seemed most strange unto my heart
That I should mourn, and thou not nigh to cheer;
That I should shrink 'mid perils, and thy spirit
Far away, far, powerless to brave them with me.
Now am I used to wear a lonesome heart
About me; now the agencies of ill
Have so oppressed my inward, absolute self,
That feelings shared, and fully answered, scarce
Would seem my own. Like a bright, singular dream
Is parted from me that strong sense of love,
Which, as one indivisible glory, lay

On both our souls, and dwelt in us, so far
As we did dwell in it. A mighty presence!
Almighty, had our wills but been confirmed
In consciousness of their immortal strength
Given by that inconceivable will eterne
For a pure birthright, when the blank of things
First owned a motive power that was not God.
But thou—thy brow has ta'en no brand of grief:
Thine eyes look cheerful, even as when we stood
By Arno, talking of the maid we loved.
In sooth I envy thee; thou seemest pure:
But I am seared: He in whom lies the world
Is coiled around the fibres of my heart,
And with his serpentine, thought-withering gaze
Doth fascinate the sovran rational eye.
There is another world: and some have deemed
It is a world of music, and of light,
And human voices, and delightful forms,
Where the material shall no more be cursed
By dominance of evil, but become
A beauteous evolution of pure spirit,
Opposite, but not warring, rather yielding
New grace, and evidence of liberty.
Oh, may we recognise each other there,
My bosom friend! May we cleave to each other
And love once more together! Pray for me,
That such may be the glory of our end.

II

A VALLEY—and a stream of purest white
Trailing its serpent form within the breast
Of that embracing dale—three sinuous hills
Imminent in calm beauty, and trees thereon,
Crest above crest, uprising to the noon,
Which dallies with their topmost tracery,
Like an old playmate, whose soft welcomings
Have less of ardour, because more of custom.
It is an English scene: and yet, methinks,
Did not yon cottage dim with azure curls
Of vapour the bright air, and that neat fence
Gird in the comfort of its quiet walls,
Or did not yon gay troop of carollers
Press on the passing breeze a native rhyme,
I might have deemed me in a foreign land.
For, as I gaze, old visions of delight
That died with th' hour their parent, are reflected
From the mysterious mirror of the mind,
Mingling their forms with these, which I behold.
Nay, the old feelings in their several states
Come up before me, and entwine with these
Of younger birth in strangest unity.
And yet who bade them forth? Who spake to Time,
That he should strike the fetters from his slaves?
Or hath he none? Is the drear prison-house
To which, 'twould seem, our spiritual acts

Pass one by one, a phantom—a dim mist
Enveloping our sphere of agency?
A guess, which we do hold for certainty?
I do but mock me with these questionings.
Dark, dark, yea, 'irrecoverably dark,'
Is the soul's eye: yet how it strives and battles
Through th' impenetrable gloom to fix
That master light, the secret truth of things,
Which is the body of the infinite God.

III

DEEP firmament, which art a voice of God,
Speak in thy mystic accents, speak yet once:
For thou *hast* spoken, and in such clear tone,
That still the sweetness murmurs thro' my soul.
Speak once again: with ardent orisons
Oft have I worshipped thee, and still I bow,
With reverence, and a feeling, like to hope,
Though something worn in th' heart, by which
we pray.
Oh, since I last beheld thee in thy pomp
Right o'er the Siren city of the south,
Rude grief and harsher sin have dealt on me
The malice of their terrible impulses;
And in a withering dream my soul has lived,
Far from the love that lieth on thy front,
As native there; far from the poesies
Which are the effluence of thy holy calm.
Thou too art changed; and that perennial light

Which there a limitless dominion held,
In fitful breaks doth shoot along yon mist,
And trembles at its own dissimilar pureness.
Yet is thy bondage beautiful ; the clouds
Drink beauty from the spirit of thy forms,
Yea, from the sacred orbits borrow grace,
To modulate their wayward phantasies.
But they are trifles : in thyself alone,
And the suffusion of thy starry light,
Firmly abide in their concordant joy,
Beauty, and music, and primeval love :
And thence may man learn an imperial truth,
That duty is the being of the soul,
And in that form alone can freedom move.
Such is your mighty language, lights of Heaven :
Oh, thrill me with its plenitude of sound,
Make me to feel, not talk of, sovranty,
And harmonise my spirit with my God !

IV

I LAY within a little bowered nook,
With all green leaves, nothing but green around
me,
And through their delicate comminglings flashed
The broken light of a sunned waterfall—
Ah, water of such freshness, that it was
A marvel and an envy ! There I lay,
And felt the joy of life for many an hour.
But when the revel of sensations

Gave place to meditation and discourse,
I waywardly began to moralise
That little theatre with its watery scene
Into quaint semblances of higher things.
And first methought that twinèd foliage
Each leaf from each how different, yet all
stamped
With common hue of green, and similar form,
Pictured in little the great human world.
Sure we are leaves of one harmonious bower,
Fed by a sap, that never will be scant,
All-permeating, all-producing mind;
And in our several parcellings of doom
We but fulfil the beauty of the whole.
Oh madness! if a leaf should dare complain
Of its dark verdure, and aspire to be
The gayer, brighter thing that wantons near.
Then as I looked
On the pure presence of that tumbling stream,
Pure amid thwarting stones and staining earth,
Oh Heaven! methought how hard it were to find
A human bosom of such stubborn truth,
Yet tempered so with yielding courtesy.
Then something rose within my heart to say—
'Maidenly virtue is the beauteous face
Which this clear glass gives out so prettily:
Maidenly virtue, born of privacy,
Lapt in a still conclusion and reserve;
Yet, when the envious winter-time is come
That kills the flaunting blossoms all arow,

If that perforce her steps must be abroad,
Keeps, like that stream, a queenly haviour,
Free from all taint of that she treads upon ;
And like those hurrying atoms in their fall,
A maiden's thoughts may dare the eye of day
To look upon their sweet sincerity.'
With that I struck into a different strain :—
'Oh ye wild atomies, whose headlong life
Is but an impulse and coaction,
Whose course hath no beginning, no, nor end ;
Are ye not weary of your mazèd whirls,
Your tortuous deviations, and the strife
Of your opposèd bubblings? Are there not
In you, as in all creatures, quiet moods,
Deep longings for a slumber and a calm?
I never saw a bird was on the wing
But with a homeward joy he seem'd to fly
As knowing all his toils' o'er-paid reward
Was with his chirpers in their little nest.
Pines have I seen on Jura's misty height,
Swinging amid the whirl-blasts of the North,
And shaking their old heads with laugh prolonged,
As if they joyed to share the mighty life
Of elements—the freedom, and the stir.
But when the gale was past, and the rent air
Returned, and the piled clouds rolled out of view,
How still th' interminable forest then !
Soundless, but for the myriad forest flies,
That hum a busy little life away

I' th' amplitude of those unstartled glades.
Why what a rest was there! But ye, oh ye!
Poor aliens from the fixed vicissitudes,
That alternate throughout created things,
Mocked with incessantness of motion,
Where shall ye find or changement or repose?'
So spake I in the fondness of my mood.
But thereat Fancy sounded me a voice
Borne upward from that sparkling company:
'Repinement dwells not with the duteous free.
We do th' Eternal Will; and in that doing,
Subject to no seducement or oppose,
We owe a privilege, that reasoning man
Hath no true touch of.' At that reproof the tears
Flushed to mine eyes; and I arose, and walked
With a more earnest and reverent heart
Forth to the world, which God had made so fair,
Mired now with trails of error and of sin.

V

(*Written in view of Ben Lomond*)

MOUNTAIN austere, and full of kinglihood!
Forgive me if, a child of later earth,
I come to bid thee hail. My days are brief,
And like the mould that crumbles on thy verge,
A minute's blast may shake me into dust;

But thou art of the things that never fail.
Before the mystic garden, and the fruit
Sung by that Shepherd-Ruler vision-blest,
Thou wert ; and from thy speculative height
Beheld'st the forms of other living souls.
Oh, if thy dread original were not sunk
I' th' mystery of universal birth,
What joy to know thy tale of mammoths huge,
And formings rare of the material prime,
And terrible craters, cold a cycle since !
To know if then, as now, thy base was laved
With moss-dark waters of a placid lake ;
If then, as now,
In the clear sunlight of thy verdant sides
Spare islets of uncertain shadow lay.

VI

It is a thing of trial to the heart,
Of trial and of painful wonderment,
To walk within a dear companion's voice
And hear him speak light words of one we hold
In the same compass of undoubting love.
'How is it that his presence being one,
His language one, his customs uniform,
He bears not the like honour in the thought
Of this my friend, which he hath borne in mine.
It minds me of that famous Arab tale
(First to expand the struggling notions
Of my child-brain) in which the bold poor man

Was checked for lack of "Open sesame."
Seems it my comrade standeth at the door
Of that rich treasure-house, my lover's heart,
Trying with keys untrue the rebel wards,
And all for lack of one unsounded word
To open out the sympathetic mind.'
Thus might a thoughtful man be eloquent,
To whom that cross had chanced : yet not such
The colour, though the nature was the same,
Of the plain fact which won me to this muse.
One morn, while in * * * I sojourned,
That winsome lady sitting by my side,
Whom still these eyes in every place desire,
We looked in quiet unison of joy
On a bright summer scene. Aspiring trees
Circled us, each in several dignity,
Yet taking, like a band of senators,
Most grandeur from their congregated calm.
Afar between two leafy willow stems
Visibly flowed the sun-lit Clyde : more near
An infant sister frolicked on the lawn,
And in sweet accents of a far-off land,
Native to th' utterer, called upon her nurse
To help her steps unto us : nor delayed
Those tones to rouse within our inmost hearts
Clear images of a delightful past.
Capri's blue distance, Procida, and the light
Pillowed on Baiæ's wave : nor less the range
Of proud Albano, backed by Puglian snows,
And the green tract beside the Lateran

Rose in me, and a mist came o'er my eyes :
But I spoke freely of these things to her,
And for awhile we walked 'mid phantom shapes
In a fair universe of other days.
That converse passed away, and careless talk,
As is its use, brought divers fancies up,
Like bubbles dancing down their rivulet
A moment, then dilating into froth.
At last, a chance-direction being given,
I spake of Wordsworth, of that lofty mind,
Enthronised in a little monarchy
Of hills and waters, where no one thing is,
Lifeless, or pulsing fresh with mountain strength,
But pays a tribute to his shaping spirit !
Thereat the lady laughed—a gentle laugh ;
For all her moods were gentle : passing sweet
Are the rebukes of woman's gentleness !
But still she laughed, and asked me how long since
I grew a dreamer, heretofore not wont
To conjure nothings to a mighty size,
Or see in Nature more than Nature owns.
Then taking up the volume, where it lay
Upon her table, of those hallowed songs,
I answered not but by their utterance.
And first the tales of quiet tenderness
(Sweet votive offerings of a loving life)
In which the feeling dignifies the fact,
I read ; then gradual rising as that sprite

Indian, by recent fabler sung so well,*
Clomb the slow column up to Seva's throne,
I opened to her view his lofty thought
More and more struggling with its walls of clay,
And on all objects of our double nature,
Inward, and outward, shedding holier light,
Till disenthralled at length it soared amain
In the pure regions of th' Eternal Same,
Where nothing meets the eye but only God.
Then spoke I of that intimate belief
In which he nursed his spirit aquiline,
How all the moving phantasies of things,
And all our visual notions, shadow-like,
Half hide, half show, that All-sustaining One,
Whose Bibles are the leaves of lowly flowers,
And the calm strength of mountains ; rippling lakes,
And the irregular howl of stormful seas ;
Soft slumbering lights of even and of morn,
And the unfolding of the star-lit gloom ;
But whose chief presence, whose imparted self
Is in the silent virtues of the heart,
The deep, the human heart, which with the high
Still glorifies the humble, and delights
To seek in every show a soul of good.
Pausing from that high strain I looked to her
For sympathy, for my full heart was up
And I would fain have felt another's breast

---

* See Southey's *Kehama.*

Mix its quick heavings with my own : indeed
The lady laughed not now, nor breathed re-
proach,
Yet there was chillness in her calm approve,
Which with my kindled temper suited not.
Oh ! there is union, and a tie of blood
With those who speak unto the general mind,
Poets and sages ! Their high privilege
Bids them eschew succession's changefulness,
And, like eternals, equal influence
Shed on all times and places. I would be
A poet, were't but for this linked delight,
This consciousness of noble brotherhood,
Whose joy no heaps of earth can bury up,
No worldly venture minish or destroy,
For it is higher, than to be personal !
Some minutes passed me by in dubious maze
Of meditation lingering painfully,
But then a calm grew on me, and clear faith
(So clear that I did marvel how before
I came not to the level of that truth)
That different halts, in Life's sad pilgrimage,
With different minstrels charm the journeying
soul.
Not in our early love's idolatry,
Not in our first ambition's flush of hope,
Not while the pulse beats high within our veins,
Fix we our soul on beautiful regrets,
Or strive to build the philosophic mind.
But when our feelings coil upon themselves

At time's rude pressure ; when the heart grows dry,
And burning with immedicable thirst,
As though a plague-spot seared it, while the brain
Fevers with cogitations void of love,
When this change comes, as come it will to most,
It is a blessed God-given aid to list
Some master's voice, speaking fiom out those depths
Of reason that do border on the source
Of pure emotion and of generous act.
It may be that this motive swayed in me,
And thinking so that day I prayed that she
Whose face, like an unruffled mountain tarn,
Smiled on me till its innocent joy grew mine,
Might ne'er experience any change of mood
So dearly bought by griefs habitual ;
Much rather, if no softer path be found
To bring our steps together happily,
Serve the bright Muses at a separate shrine.

1829.

TIMBUCTOO

Be Yarrow stream unseen, unknown!
It must, or we shall rue it:
We have a vision of our own;
Ah! why should we undo it?
WORDSWORTH.

THERE was a land, which, far from human sight,
Old Ocean compassed with his numerous waves,
In the lone West. Tenacious of her right,
Imagination decked those unknown caves,
And vacant forests, and clear peaks of ice
With a transcendent beauty; that which saves
From the world's blight our primal sympathies,
Still in man's heart, as some familiar shrine,
Feeding the tremulous lamp of love that never dies.
Poets have loved that land, and dared to twine
Round its existence memories of old time,
When the good reigned; and none in grief did pine.
Sages, and all who owned the might sublime
To impress their thought upon the face of things,
And teach a nation's spirit how to climb,

Spake of long-lost Atlantis,* when the springs
Of clear Ilissus or the Tusculan bower
Were welcoming the pure rest which Wisdom brings
To her elect, the marvellous calm of power.
Oft, too, some maiden, garlanding her brow
With Baian roses, at eve's mystic hour,
Has gazed on the sun's path, as he sank low,
I' th' awful main, behind Inarime ;†
And with clasped hands, and gleaming eye, 'Shalt thou,
First-born of light, endure in the flat sea
Such intermission of thy life intense?
Thou lordly one, is there no home for thee?'
A youth took up the voice: 'Thou speedest hence,
Beautiful orb, but not to death or sleep,
That feel we ; worlds invisible to sense,
Whose course is pure, where eyes forget to weep,
And th' earthly sisterhood of sorrow and love
Some god putteth asunder, these shall keep

* The legend of the lost continent Atlantis is so well known, and its derivation from an early knowledge of America seems so natural and probable, that, had not this poem been pretty generally censured for its obscurity, I should have thought a note on the subject superfluous. In the beautiful opening of the *Timaeus*, Plato has alluded to a form of this legend highly creditable to the Athenians, which will serve to show the notions entertained of the extent and relative importance of Atlantis.

† Inarime, now the island of Ischia.

Thy state imperial now: there shalt thou move
  Fresh hearts with warmth and joyance to
    rebound,
  By many a musical stream and solemn
    grove.'
Years lapsed in silence, and that holy ground
  Was still an Eden, shut from sight, and few
  Brave souls in its idea solace found.
In the last days a man arose, who knew*
  That ancient legend from his infancy.
  Yea, visions on that child's emmarvailed view
Had flashed intuitive science; and his glee
  Was lofty as his pensiveness, for both
  Wore the bright colours of the thing to be!
But when his prime of life was come, the wrath
  Of the cold world fell on him; it did thrill
  His inmost self, but never quenched his faith.

---

* These lines were suggested to me by the following passage in Mr. Coleridge's *Friend*: 'It cannot be deemed alien from the purposes of this disquisition, if we are anxious to attract the attention of our readers to the importance of this speculative meditation, even for the worldly interests of mankind; and to that concurrence of nature and historic event with the great revolutionary movements of individual genius, of which so many instances occur in the study of history, how nature (why should we hesitate in saying, that which in nature itself is more than nature?) seems to come forward in order to meet, to aid, and to reward every idea excited by a contemplation of her methods in the spirit of a filial care, and with the humility of love.'—*Friend*, vol. iii. p. 190. Mr. Coleridge proceeds to illustrate this by the very example of Columbus, and quotes some highly beautiful and applicable verses of *Chiabrera*.

Still to that faith he added search, and still,
As fevering with fond love of th' unknown shore,
From learning's fount he strove his thirst to fill.
But always Nature seemed to meet the power
Of his high mind, to aid, and to reward
His reverent hope with her sublimest lore.
Each sentiment that burned; each falsehood warred
Against and slain; each novel truth in-wrought—
What were they, but the living lamps that starred
His transit o'er the tremulous gloom of Thought?
More, and now more, their gathered brilliancy
On the one master Notion sending out,
Which brooded ever o'er the passionate sea
Of his deep soul; but ah! too dimly seen,
And formless in its own immensity!
Last came the joy, when that phantasmal scene
Lay in full glory round his outward sense;
And who had scorned before in hatred keen
Refuged their baseness now: for no pretence
Could wean their souls from awe; they dared not doubt
That with them walked on earth a spirit in-tense.
So others trod his path: and much was wrought
In the new land, that made the angels weep.

That innocent blood—it was not shed for
nought!
My God! it is an hour of dread, when leap
Like a fire-fountain forth the energies
Of Guilt, and desolate the poor man's sleep.
Yet not alone for torturing agonies,
Though meriting most, nor all that storm of
Woe
Which did entempest their pure fulgent skies,
Shall the deep curse of ages cling, and grow
To the foul names of those who did the
deed,
The lusters for the gold of Mexico!
Mute are th' ancestral voices we did heed,
The tones of superhuman melody:
And the 'veiled maid'* is vanished, who did
feed

---

* These lines contain an allusion to that magnificent passage in Mr. Shelley's *Alastor*, where he describes 'the spirit of sweet Human Love' descending in vision on the slumbers of the wandering poet. How far I have a right to transfer the 'veiled maid' to my own Poem, where she must stand for the embodiment of that love for the unseen, that voluntary concentration of our vague ideas of the Beauty that *ought* to be, on some one spot, or country yet undiscovered, as in the instances I have chosen, on America or the African city, this the critics, if I have any, may determine. I shall, however, be content to have trespassed against the commandments of Art, if I should have called any one's attention to that wonderful Poem, which cannot long remain in its present condition of neglect, but which, when it shall have emerged into the light, its inheritance, will produce wonder and enthusiastic delight in thousands, who will

By converse high the faith of liberty
  In young unwithered hearts, and Virtue, and
    Truth,
  And every thing that makes us joy to Be!
Lo! there hath past away a glory of Youth
  From this our world; and all is common now,
  And sense doth tyrannise o'er Love and Ruth.
What, is Hope dead? and gaze we her pale brow,
  Like the cold statues round a Roman's bier,
  Then tearless travel on through tracts of
    human woe?
No! there is one, one ray that lingers here,
  To battle with the world's o'ershadowing form,
  Like the last firefly of a Tuscan year,

---

learn, as the work, like every perfect one, grows upon them, that the deep harmonies and glorious imaginations in which it is clothed, are not more true than the great moral idea which is its permeating life. The lines alluded to are these:—

'The poet wandering on, through Arabie
And Persia, and the wild Carmanian waste,
And o'er the aërial mountains which pour down
Indus and Oxus from their icy caves,
In joy and exultation held his way;
Till in the vale of Cachmire, far within
Its loneliest dell, where odorous plants entwine
Beneath the hollow rocks a natural bower,
Beside a sparkling rivulet he stretched
His languid limbs. A vision on his sleep
There came, a dream of hopes that never yet
Had flushed his cheek. He dreamed a veiled maid
Sate near him, talking in low solemn tones.
Her voice was like the voice of his own soul,
Heard in the calm of thought: its music long,

Or dying flashes of a noble storm.
  Beyond the clime of Tripoly, and beyond
  Bahr Abiad, where the lone peaks, unconform
To other hills, and with rare foliage crowned,
  Hold converse with the Moon, a City stands
  Which yet no mortal guest hath ever found.
Around it stretch away the level sands
  Into the silence : pausing in his course,
  The ostrich kens it from his subject lands.
Here with faint longings and a subdued force,
  Once more was sought th' ideal aliment
  Of Man's most subtle being, the prime source
Of all his blessings : here might still be blent
  Whate'er of heavenly beauty in form or sound,
  Illumes the Poet's heart with ravishment.

Like woven sounds of streams and breezes, held
His inmost sense suspended in its web
Of many-coloured woof and shifting hues.
Knowledge and Truth and Virtue were her theme,
And lofty hopes of divine liberty,
Thoughts the most dear to him, and poesy,
Herself a poet. Soon the solemn mood
Of her pure mind kindled through all her frame
A permeating fire : wild numbers then
She raised with voice stifled with tremulous sobs
Subdued by its own pathos : her fair hands
Were bare alone, sweeping from some strange harp
Strange symphony, and in her branching veins
The eloquent blood told an ineffable tale :
The beating of her heart was heard to fill
The pauses of her music, and her breath
Tumultuously accorded with those fits
Of intermitted song.'

Thou fairy City, which the desert mound
  Encompasseth, thou alien from the mass
  Of human guilt, I would not wish thee found!
Perchance thou art too pure, and dost surpass
  Too far amid th' Ideas rangèd high
  In the Eternal Reason's perfectness,
To our deject, and most imbasèd eye
  To look unharmed on thine integrity,
  Symbol of Love, and Truth, and all that cannot die.
Thy palaces and pleasure-domes to me
  Are matter of strange thought: for sure thou art
  A splendour in the wild: and aye to thee
Did visible guardians of the Earth's great heart
  Bring their choice tributes, culled from many a mine,
  Diamond, and jasper, porphyry, and the art
Of figured chrysolite: nor silver shine
  There wanted, nor the mightier power of gold:
  So wert thou reared of yore, City divine.
And who are they of blisses manifold,
  That dwell within thee? Spirits of delight,
  It may be spirits whose pure thoughts enfold,
In eminence of Being, all the light
  That interpenetrates this mighty All,
  And doth endure in its own beauty's right.
And oh! the vision were majestical
  To them, indeed, of column, and of spire,
  And hanging garden, and hoar waterfall!

For we, poor prisoners of this earthy mire,
See little; they the essence and the law
Robing each thing in its peculiar tire.
Yet moments have been, when in thought I saw
That city rise upon me from the void,
Populous with men: and phantasy would draw
Such portraiture of life, that I have joyed
In over-measure to behold her work,
Rich with the myriad charms, by evil unalloyed.
Methought I saw a nation, which did hark
To Justice, and to Truth: their ways were strait,
And the dread shadow, Tyranny, did lurk
Nowhere about them: not to scorn, or hate
A living thing was their sweet nature's bond:
So every soul moved free in kingly state.
Suffering they had (nor else were virtue found
In these our pilgrim spirits): gently still
And as from cause external came the wound,
Not like a gangrene of soul-festering ill,
To taint the springs of life, and undermine
The holy strength of their majestic Will.
Methought I saw a face whose every line
Wore the pale cast of Thought;* a good, old man,

---

* These characters are of course purely ideal, and meant to show, by way of particular diagram, that right temperament

Most eloquent, who spake of things divine.
Around him youths were gathered, who did scan
His countenance so grand and mild; and drank
The sweet, sad tones of Wisdom, which outran
The life-blood, coursing to the heart, and sank
Inward from thought to thought, till they abode
'Mid Being's dim foundations, rank by rank
With those transcendent truths, arrayed by God
In linkèd armour for untiring fight,
Whose victory is, where time hath never trod.
Methought I saw a maiden in the light
Of beauty musing near an amaranth bower,
Herself a lordly blossom. Past delight
Was fused in actual sorrow by the power
Of mightiest Love upon her delicate cheek;
And magical was her wailing at that hour.
For aye with passionate sobs she mingled meek
Smiles of severe content: as though she raised
To Him her inmost heart, who shields the weak.

---

of the intellect and the heart which I have assigned to this favoured nation. I cannot, however, resist the pleasure of declaring that, in the composition of the lines, 'Methought I saw,' etc., my thoughts dwelt almost involuntarily on those few conversations which it is my delight to have held with that 'good old man, most eloquent,' Samuel Coleridge.

She wept not long in solitude: I gazed,
Till women, and sweet children came, and took
Her hand, and uttered meaning words, and praised
The absent one with eyes, which as a book
Revealed the workings of the heart sincere.
In sooth it was a glorious thing to look
Upon that interchange of smile and tear!
But when the mourner turned, in innocent grace
Lifting that earnest eye and forehead clear,
Oh then, methought, God triumphed in her face!
But these are dreams: though ministrant on good,
Dreams are they; and the Night of things their place.
So be it ever! Ever may the mood
'In which the affections gently lead us on'*
Be as thy sphere of visible life. The crowd,
The turmoil, and the countenances wan
Of slaves, the Power-inchanted, thou shalt flee,
And by the gentle heart be seen, and loved alone.

June, 1829.

* Wordsworth's *Tintern Abbey*.

SONETTO

*Alla Statua, Ch' e a Firenze di Lorenzo
Duca D'Urbino, Scolta da Michaelangiolo.*

DEH, chi se' tu, ch' in sì superba pietra
Guardi, e t' accigli, più che creatura?
La maestà della fronte alta, e pura,
L'occhio, ch' appena il duro marmo arretra
L'agevol man, da cui bel velo impetra
La mossa de pensier profonda, e scura,
Dicon: 'Questi é Lorenzo, e se pur dura
Suo nome ancor, questo il Destino spetra'
Tosca magion—ahi vituperio ed onta
Della nobil città, che l'Arno infiora,
Qual danno fé de vostre palle il suono!
Pure innanzi a beltade ira tramonta:
E Fiorenza, ch' l giogo ange, e scolora,
Dice ammirando, 'Oimè! quas' io perdono!'

ROME, *December*, 1827.

SONETTO

GENOVA bella, a cui l' altiera voce*
Di costanza e virtù feo grande onore,
Allorchè rossegiò quel tristo albore,
Pien di spaventi, e gridi, e guasto atroce
E'l fiume ostil, che mai non mise foce
Nel dolce suol, che della terra è fiore,
Piagava sì, ma non vincea quel core.
Or che ti resta? Or dov' é la feroce
Antica mente? E Lei—tra pene, e guai
L'invitta Liberta—qual rupe or serba?
Forse (oh pensier!) qui volge il passo omai,
E freme, e tace; o con dolcezza acerba
Dice, oscurando del bel viso i rai,
'Com' è caduta la città superba!'

December, 1827.

---

*Alluding to the Sonnet of Passerini, beginning 'Genova mia.' It is in the *Componimento Lirici* of Mathias.

TO AN ENGLISH LADY

('Tra bella e buona non so qual fosse piu')

Who not having fulfilled her promise to meet me at a Roman festival, sent me a note requesting pardon.

Ahi vera donna ! or dal tessuto inganno
  Riconosco, chi sei : la gran vaghezza
  Ch' angelica mi parve, or fugge, e spezza
  Quel caro laccio di soave affanno.
Collo, ch' i neri anelli un marmo fanno,
  Trecce, che più di sè l'anima apprezza,
  E voi, begli occhi di fatal dolcezza,
  Che feci io mai per meritar tal danno?
Tu pur, notte spietata, or vieni, e dille
  (Chè senza testimon nol crederia)
  Com' io guardava a mille visi, e mille,
E dicea, sospirando, in fioco suono,
  'Mille non sono, quel ch' una saria'—
  Va, traditrice, e non sperar perdono.

Rome, *Jan.* 1828.

SONETTO

(*Scritto sul Lago d'Albano*)

SOAVE venticel ch' intorno spiri,
  Or cogli elci scherzando, or sulle sponde
  Destando il mormorar di lucid' onde,
  Deh non tardar, non più frenar tuoi giri.
Vattene innanzi, e là 've giuso ammiri
  Un fiorellin, che dall' amena fronde
  Gioia, e dolcezza in ogni seno infonde,
  China le piume, e dille i miei sospiri.
Quanta invidia ti porto! In sul bel volto
  Lente isvolazzi, e baci quel natio
  Aureo sorriso, cui veder m'è tolto!
Fossi pur teco! Ahi quale tremolio
  Al cor darebbe il trastullarmi avvolto
  Ne' cari lacci, e il susurrar 'Sonio!'

March, 1828.

SONETTO

ON A LADY SUFFERING SEVERE ILLNESS

(*Imitated from the English*)

PIETÀ ! Pietà ! gran Dio ! deh, volgi omai
L'impietosito sguardo : il bel sembiante
Le luci giovanette, e vaghe, e sante,
Non mertan, no, soffrir dell' empio i guai.
'Mortal, mortal, che delirando vai,'
Ripose quel del trono sfolgorante,
'Ve' com' ogni dolor par che si schiante
'A' puri di gran Fede augusti rai.'
'Alma beata è questa ! E se pur l'ange
'Nel fior degli anni suoi cotanta pena,
To la sostengo ; e questa man la mena !'
Cosi lo spirto umil, cui nulla frange,
(O speme di virtù salda, e serena !)
Beve l'amaro nappo, e mai non piange.

ROME, *April*, 1828.

SONETTO

ALLA SIRENA, NUME AVITO DI NAPOLI

(*Scritto in Tirolo*)

DONNA di gran poter, ch' il colle adorno
  Molci regina, u' sospirar non lice,
  Fuori ch' ai dolci lai, che d'ogni intorno
  S' odon nell' ombra de' gran vati altrice,
Deh vieni, oh tu sì bella—e senza scorno
  (Pietà per fermo a niuna dea disdice)
  Favellami di lei, ch'il tuo soggiorno
  Par faccia più ridente, e più felice.
Misero, che ragiono? il suon risponde
  D'Euro ululando tra l'Alpina foglia;
  Tu pur ti stai lontana—e fai gran senno;
Che se'l tuo vol piegassi ad ogni cenno
  Ch' ad or, ad or, manda l'atroce doglia,
  Lungi da lei verresti a torbid' onde!

May, 1828.

SONNET

ON THE PICTURE OF THE THREE FATES IN THE PALAZZO PITTI AT FLORENCE, USUALLY ASCRIBED TO MICHELANGIOLO

NONE but a Tuscan hand could fix ye here
In rigidness of sober colouring.
Pale are ye, mighty Triad, not with fear,
But the most awful knowledge, that the spring
Is in you of all birth, and act, and sense.
I sorrow to behold ye: pain is blent
With your aloof and loveless permanence,
And your high princedom seems a punishment.
The cunning limner could not personate
Your blind control, save in th' aspect of grief;
So does the thought repugn of sovran Fate.
Let him gaze here who trusts not in the love
Toward which all being solemnly doth move:
More this grand sadness tells, than forms of fairest life.

TO MALEK

MALEK, the counsel of thine amity
  I slight not, kindly tendered, but rejoice
  To hear or praise or censure from thy voice,
  Both for thy sake, and hers, whose spirit in
      thee
Indwelleth ever, starlike Poesy!
  Woe, if I pass the temple of her choice
  With reckless step, or th' unexpressive joys
  Disdain of Fancy, pure to song, and free!
Yet deem not thou thy friend of early days
  So lost to high emprize: trust me his soul
  Sleeps not the dreamless sleep, which thou
      art fearing.
No! still on lights the love of noble praise
  His pilgrim bark, like a clear star appearing:
  And oh, how bright that beam, where storm-
      waves roll!

June, 1828.

SONNET

OH blessing and delight of my young heart,
Maiden, who was so lovely and so pure,
I know not in what region now thou art,
Or whom thy gentle eyes in joy assure.
Not the old hills on which we gazed together,
Not the old faces which we both did love,
Not the old books, whence knowledge we did gather,
Not these, but others now thy fancies move.
I would I knew thy present hopes and fears,
All thy companions, with their pleasant talk,
And the clear aspect which thy dwelling wears:
So, though in body absent, I might walk
With thee in thought and feeling, till thy mood
Did sanctify mine own to peerless good.

April, 1829.

SONNET

(*Written in Edinburgh*)

EVEN thus, methinks, a city reared should be!
  Yea, an imperial city, that might hold
  Five times a hundred noble towns in fee,
  And either with their might of Babel old,
Or the rich Roman pomp of empery
  Might stand compare, highest in arts enroll'd,
  Highest in arms; brave tenement for the free,
  Who never crouch to thrones, or sin for gold.
Thus should her towers be raised—with vicinage
  Of clear bold hills, that curve her very streets,
  As if to vindicate 'mid choicest seats
Of art, abiding Nature's majesty,
  And the broad sea beyond, in calm or rage
  Chainless alike, and teaching Liberty.

July, 1829.

TO AN ADMIRED LADY

WHEN thou art dreaming, at the time of night
That dreams have deepest truth, comes not the
form
Of th' ancient poet near thee? Streams not light
From his immortal presence, chasing harm
From thy pure pillow, and each nocturnal sprite
Freighting with happy fancies to thy soul?
Says he not, 'Surely, maiden, my control
Shall be upon thee, for thy soul is dight
In a most clear majestic tenderness,
And natural art springs freshly from its deeps.'
Then as he clasps his reverend palms to bless
Out from the dark a gentle family leaps,
Juliet and Imogen, with many a fere,
Acclaiming all, 'Welcome, our sister dear!'

STANZAS

(Written after visiting Melrose Abbey in company of Sir Walter Scott)

I

I LIVED an hour in fair Melrose;
  It was not when 'the pale moonlight'
Its magnifying charm bestows;
  Yet deem I that I 'viewed it right.'
The wind-swept shadows fast careered,
Like living things that joyed or feared,
Adown the sunny Eildon Hill,
And the sweet winding Tweed the distance crownèd well.

II

I inly laughed to see that scene
  Wear such a countenance of youth,
Though many an age those hills were green,
  And yonder river glided smooth,
Ere in these now disjointed walls,
The Mother Church held festivals,
And full-voiced anthemings the while
Swelled from the choir, and lingered down the echoing aisle.

III

I coveted that Abbey's doom ;
  For if I thought the early flowers
Of our affection may not bloom,
  Like those green hills, through countless
      hours,
Grant me at least a tardy waning,
Some pleasure still in age's paining ;
Though lines and forms must fade away,
Still may old Beauty share the empire of Decay !

IV

But looking toward the grassy mound
  Where calm the Douglas chieftains lie,
Who, living, quiet never found,
  I straightway learnt a lesson high :
For there an old man sat serene,
And well I knew that thoughtful mien
Of him whose early lyre had thrown
Over these mould'ring walls the magic of its
      tone.

V

Then ceased I from my envying state,
  And knew that aweless intellect
Hath power upon the ways of fate,
  And works through time and space uncheckt.
That minstrel of old chivalry
In the cold grave must come to be,

But his transmitted thoughts have part
In the collective mind, and never shall depart.

VI

It was a comfort, too, to see
  Those dogs that from him ne'er would rove,
And always eyed him rev'rently,
  With glances of depending love.
They know not of that eminence
Which marks him to my reasoning sense;
They know but that he is a man,
And still to them is kind, and glads them all he
    can.

VII

And hence their quiet looks confiding,
  Hence grateful instincts seated deep,
By whose strong bond, were ill betiding,
  They'd risk their own his life to keep.
What joy to watch in lower creature
Such dawning of a moral nature,
And how (the rule all things obey)
They look to a higher mind to be their law and
    stay!

August, 1829.

STANZAS

(Written at Caudebec in Normandy)

I

WHEN life is crazy in my limbs,
  And hope is gone astray,
And in my soul's December fade
  The love-thoughts of its May,
One spot of earth is left to me
  Will warm my heart again ;
'Tis Caudebec and Mailleraie
  On the pleasant banks of Seine.

II

The dark wood's crownal on the hill,
  The river curving bright,
The graceful barks that rest, or play,
  Pure creatures of delight—
Oh, these are shows by nature given
  To warm old hearts again,
At Caudebec and Mailleraie
  On the pleasant banks of Seine.

III

The Tuscan's land, I loved it well,
  And the Switzer's clime of snow,
And many a bliss me there befell
  I never more can know;
But for quiet joy of nature's own
  To warm the heart again,
Give me Caudebec and Mailleraie
  On the pleasant banks of Seine.

June, 1829.

A FAREWELL TO GLENARBACH *

I

WHEN grief is felt along the blood,
  And checks the breath with sighs unsought,
'Tis then that Memory's power is wooed
  To sooth by ancient forms of thought.
It is not much, yet in that day
  Will seem a gladsome wakening;
And such to me, in joy's decay,
  The memory of the Roebuck Glen.

II

Nor less, when fancies have their bent,
  And eager passion sweeps the mind;
'Twill bless to catch a calm content
  From happy moment far behind.
Oh, it is of a heavenly brood
  That chast'ning recollection!
And such to me, in joyous mood,
  The memory of the Roebuck Glen.

* The Glen of the Roebuck.

III

I grieve to quit this lime-tree walk,
  The Clyde, the Leven's milder blue
To lose ; yon craigs that nest the hawk
  Will soar no longer in my view.
Yet of themselves small power to move
  Have they : their light 's a borrowed thing
Won from her eyes, for whom I love
  The memory of the Roebuck Glen.

IV

Oh, dear to nature, not in vain
  The mountain winds have breathed on thee !
Mild virtues of a noble strain,
  And beauty making pure and free,
Pass to thee from the silent hills :
  And hence, where'er thy sojourning,
Thine eye with gentle weeping fills
  At memory of the Roebuck Glen.

V

Thou speedest to the sunny shore,
  Where first thy presence on me shone ;
Alas ! I know not whether more
  These eyes shall claim thee as their own :
But should a kindly star prevail,
  And should we meet far hence again,
How sweet in other lands to hail
  The memory of the Roebuck Glen.

VI

Oh, when the thought comes o'er my heart
  Of happy meetings yet to be,
The very feeling that thou art
  Is deep as that of life to me;
Yet should sad instinct in my breast
  Speak true, and darker chance obtain,
Bless with one tear my final rest,
  One memory from the Roebuck Glen.

July, 1829.

STANZAS

(*Written on the Banks of the Tay*)

I

I SAW a child upon a Highland moor,
  Playing with heath-flowers in her gamesome mood,
And singing snatches wild of Gaelic lore,
  That thrilled like witch-notes my susceptive blood.
I spake a Southern word, but not the more
  Did she regard or move from where she stood.
It seemed the business of her life to play
With euphrasies and bluebells day by day.

II

Then my first thought was of the joy to grow
  With her, and like her, as a mountain plant,
That to one spot attached doth bud and blow,
  Then, in the rains of autumn, leaves to vaunt
Its fragrance to the air, and sinks, till low
  Winter consign it, like a satiate want,
To the earth's endearment, who will fondly nourish
The loosèd substance, until spring reflourish

III

'To be thy comrade, and thy brother, maiden,
To chaunt with thee the antique song I hear,
Joying the joy that looks not toward its fading,
The sweet philosophy of young life's cheer!
We should be like two bees with honey laden,
Or two blithe butterflies a rose-tree near!'—
So I went dreaming how to play a child
Once more with her who 'side me sang and smiled.

IV

Then a stern knowledge woke along my soul,
And sudden I was sadly made aware
That childish joy is now a folded scroll,
And new ordainments have their several fair:
When evening lights press the ripe greening knoll,
True heart will never wish the morning there:
Where archèd boughs enlace the golden light,
Did ever poet pray for franchised sight.

V

When we were children, we did sigh to reach
The eminence of a man; yet in our thought,
And in the prattled fancies of our speech,
It was a baby-man we fashioned out;

And now that childhood seems the only leech
  For all the heartaches of a rough world caught,
Sooth is, we wish to be a twofold thing,
And keep our present self to watch within.

July, 1829.

STANZAS

ON MY SISTER'S BIRTHDAY

(Written at Callander, near Loch Katrine)

I

FAIR fall the day! 'Tis thirteen years
  Since on this day was Ellen born,
And shed the dark world's herald tears
  On such another summer's morn.
I may not hear her laughter's flow,
  Nor watch the smile upon her face,
But in my heart I surely know
  There's joy within her dwelling-place.

II

Oh, at the age of fair thirteen
  A birthday is a thing of power:
The meadows wear a livelier green,
  Be it a time of sun, or shower;
We scarce believe the robin's note
  Unborrowed from the nightingale,
And when the sweet long day is out,
  Our dreams take up the merry tale.

III

That pleasure being innocent,
With innocence alone accords :
The souls that Passion's strife has rent
Have other thoughts and other words ;
They cannot bear that meadow's green ;
Strange grief is in the robin's song ;
And when they hope to shift the scene,
Their dreams the anguish but prolong.

IV

Oh, pray for them, thou happy child,
Whose souls are in that silent woe ;
For once like thee, they gaily smiled,
And hoped, and feared and trusted so !
Pray for them in thy birthday mood,
They may not pass that awful bar,
Which separates the early good
From spirits with themselves at war.

V

Their mind is now on loves grown cold,
On friendships falling slow away,
On life lived fast, and heart made old
Before a single hair was grey.
Or should they be one thought less sad,
Their dream is still of things foregone,
Sweet scenes that once had made them glad,
Dim faces seen, and never known.

VI

My own dear sister, thy career
  Is all before thee, thorn and flower ;
Scarce hast thou known by joy or fear
  The still heart-pride of Friendship's hour :
And for that awful thing beyond,
  The first affection's going forth,
In books alone thy sighs have owned
  The heaven, and then the hell, on earth

VII

But time is rolling onward, love,
  And birthdays one another chace ;
Ah, when so much few years remove,
  May thy sweet nature hold its place—
Who would not hope, who would not pray,
  That looks on thy demeanour now ?
Yet have I seen the slow decay
  Of many souls as pure as thou.

VIII

But there are some whose light endures—
  A sign of wonder, and of joy,
Which never custom's mist obscures,
  Or passion's treacherous gust destroy.
God make with them a rest for thee !
  For thou art turned toward stormy seas,
And when they call thee like to me,
  Some terrors on my bosom seize.

IX

Yet why to-day this mournful tone,
  When thou on gladness hast a claim?
How ill befits a boding moan
  From one who bears a brother's name!
Here fortune, fancifully kind,
  Has led me to a lovely spot,
Where not a tree or rock I find,
  My sister, that recalls thee not!

X

Benan is worth a poet's praise;
  Bold are the cairns of Benvenue;
Most beautiful the winding ways
  Where Trossachs open on the view:
But other grace Loch Katrine wears,
  When viewed by me from Ellen's Isle;
A magic tint on all appears;
  It comes from thy remembered smile!

XI

'Twas there that Lady of the Lake
  Moored to yon gnarled tree her boat,
And where FitzJames's horn bade wake
  Each mountain echo's lengthened note;
'Twas from that slope the maiden heard:
  Sweet tale! but sweeter far to me,
From dreamy blendings of that word,
  With all my thoughts and hopes of thee.

3rd August, 1829.

FROM SCHILLER

(*Written at Malvern*)

I

To yonder vale where shepherds dwell,
  There came with every dawning year,
Ere earliest larks their notes did trill,
  A lady wonderful and fair.

II

She was not born within that vale,
  And none from whence she came might know,
But soon all trace of her did fail,
  Whene'er she turned her, far to go.

III

But blessing was when she was seen :
  All hearts that day were beating high :
A holy calm was in her mien,
  And queenly glanced her maiden eye.

IV

She brought with her both fruits and flowers
  Were gathered in another clime,
Beneath a different sun from ours,
  And in a nature more sublime.

V

To each and all a gift she gave,
  And one had fruit, and one had flower ;
Nor youth, nor old man with his stave,
  Did homeward go without his dower.

VI

So all her welcome guests were glad—
  But most rejoiced one loving pair,
Who took of her the best she had,
  The brightest blooms that ever were !

Sept. 1829.

LINES SPOKEN IN THE CHARACTER OF PYGMALION

(Written on the occasion of a represented Charade)

'TIS done, the work is finished—that last touch
Was as a God's! Lo! now it stands before me,
Even as long years ago I dreamed of it,
Consummate offspring of consummate art;
Ideal form itself! Ye Gods, I thank you,
That I have lived to this: for this thrown off
The pleasure of my kind; for this have toiled
Days, nights, months, years;—am not I recompensed?
Who says an artist's life is not a king's?
I *am* a king, alone among the crowd
Of busy hearts and looks—apart with nature
I sit, a God upon the earth, creating
More lovely forms than flesh and blood can equal.
Jove's workmanship is perishable clay,
But mine immortal marble; when the proudest
Of our fair city dames is laid i' the dust
This creature of my soul will still be lovely.
Let me contemplate thee again. That lip—
How near it wears the crimson! and that eye—

How strives it with the marble's vacancy!
Methinks if thou wert human, I could love thee;
But that thou art not, nor wilt ever be—
Ne'er know and feel how beautiful thou art.
Oh God, I am alone then—she hears not—
And yet how like to life! Ha! blessed thought,
Gods have heard prayers ere now. Hear me, bright Venus,
Queen of my dreams, hear from thy throne of light,
Forgive the pride that made my human heart
Forget its nature. Let her live and love!
I dare not look again—my brain swims round—
I dream—I dream—even now methought she moved—
If 'tis a dream, how will I curse the dawn
That wakes me from it! There—that bend again—
It is no dream—Oh, speak to me and bless me.

1832.

TO TWO SISTERS

'Love-thoughts be rich when canopied with flowers.'
SHAKESPEARE.

[In Leigh Hunt's *Indicator* it is stated that the name 'Mary' has its origin in a Hebrew word, signifying 'Exalted'; and a suggestion occurs in the same book, that 'Emily' may possibly come from some element akin to 'Amo.']

WELL do your names express ye, sisters dear,
In small clear sounds awaking mournful thoughts,
Mournful, as with the refluence of a joy
Too pure for these sad coasts of human life.
Methinks, had not your happy vernal dawn
Ever arisen on my trancèd view,
Those flowing sounds would syllable yourselves
To my delighted soul, or if not so,
Yet when I traced their deeper meaning out,
And fathomed his intent, who in some hour,
Sweet from the world's young dawn, with breath of life
Endowed them, then your certain forms would come,
Pale but true visions of my musing eye.
For thee, Oh! eldest flower, whose precious name
Would to inspirèd ears by Chebar once,
Or the lone cavern hid from Jezebel,

Sound as 'Exalted'—fitliest, therefore, borne
By that mysterious Lady who reposed
In Egypt far, beyond the impious reach
Of fell Herodes, or the unquiet looks
Of men, who knew not Peace to earth was born,—
There happily reposed, waiting the time
When from that dark interminable day
Should by God's might emerge, and Love sit throned,
And Meekness kiss away the looks of Scorn ;
Oh ! Mary, deem that Virgin looks on thee
With an especial care ; lean thou on her,
As the ideal of thy woman's heart ;
Pray that thy heart be strengthened from above
To lasting hope, and sovran kindliness ;
That conquering smiles and more than conquering tears
May be thy portion through the ways of life :
So walk thou on in thy simplicity,
Following the Virgin Queen for evermore !
Thou other name, I turn with deepest awe
To think of all thou utterest unto me.
Oh, Emily ! how frail must be my speech,
Weighed with the thought that in my spirit burns,
To find no rest until 'tis known by thee,
Till our souls see each other face to face.
Thou hearest not, alas ! thou art afar,
And I am lone as ever, sick and lone,

Roaming the weary desert of my doom
Where thou art not, altho' all speaks of thee,
All yearns for thee, my love : each barren wold
Would teem with fruitful glory at thy smile.
But so—'twas of thy name that I would speak,
And thus I will not lend me to that lie,
That from the old and proud Æmilian clan
Thy name was brought, the famous Roman dames
Who, in a sweeping stole, broad-zoned and full,
With solemn brows and settled eyes severe,
Tended the household glory of their lords.
Ah, no ! a sweeter birth, fair name, is thine !
Surely some soul born in the tender light
Of golden suns and deep-starred night divine,
Feeling the want of some far gentler word
Than any speech doth own, to slake the thirst
Of his impetuous heart, and be at once
The symbol and relief of that high love
Which made him weary and faint even unto death,
He gathering up the wasted energies
For a last work, and breathing all his life
Into a word of love, said 'Amelie,'
Meaning 'Beloved'; and then methinks he died,
And the melodious magic of his voice
Shrank in its fulness ; but the amorous air,
And the blue sea close murmuring to the shore
With a sweet regular moan, the orange grove

TO TWO SISTERS

Rising from that slope shore in richest shade,
Blent with the spikèd aloe, and cactus wild,
And rarer growth of the luxuriant palm,
Lived in that word, and echoed 'Emily,'
Tempering the tone with variation sweet.
Thou seest it, maiden : if the fairest things
Of this fair world, and breathing deepest love,
Sang welcome to the name then framed for thee,
And such as thee, the gentlest of the earth,
Should I, to whom this tale was whispered
By some kind Muse in hours of silent thought,
Look on thy face and call thee not 'Beloved,'
It were in me unmeasured blasphemy.
Oh ! envy not thyself thy station high :
Consent to be 'Beloved' ; I ask no more
Than to fulfil for thee thy warning name,
And in a perfect loving live and die.

Nov. 1830.

This was my lay in sad nocturnal hour,
What time the silence felt a growing sound
Awful, and winds began among the trees,
Nor was there starlight in the vaulted sky.
Now is the eyelid of the jocund sun
Uplifted on the region of this air,
And in the substance of his living light
I walk enclosed, therefore to matin chaunts
Of all delighted birds I marry a note
Of human voice rejoicing unto thee,

Ever beloved, warbling my rapture now,
As erst to thee I made melodious moan.
Then I believed thee distant from my heart;
Thou hadst not spoken then, I had not heard:
And I was faint, because I breathèd not
Breath of thy love, wherein alone is life.
But at this hour my heart is seen, my prayer
Answered and crowned with blessing; I have
looked
Into thine eyes which have not turned away,
But rested all their lavish light upon me,
Unutterably sweet, till I became
Angelic in the strength of tenderness,
And met thy soul down-looking into mine
With a responsive power; thy word hath passed
Upon my spirit, and is a light for ever,
High o'er the drifting spray of circumstance.
Thy word, the plighted word, the word of pro-
mise,
And of all comfort! In its mighty strength
I bid thee hail, not as in former days,
Not as my chosen only, but my bride,
My very bride, coming to make my house
A glorious temple! Be the seal of God
Upon that word until the hour be full!

Feb. 1831.

TO THE LOVED ONE

My heart is happy now, beloved,
  Albeit thy form is far away;
A joy that will not be removed
  Broods on me like a summer's day.
Whatever evil Fate may do,
  It cannot change what has been thine;
It cannot cast those words anew,
  The gentle words I think divine.

No touch of time can blight the glance
  That blest with early hope my love;
New years are dark with fearful chance,
  That moment is with God above:
And never more from me departs
  Of that sweet time the influence rare,
When first we looked into our hearts
  And told each other what was there.

Yes, I am happy, love; and yet
  Lone cherished pain will keep a strife;
Something half fear and half regret
  Is lingering at the seat of life.

But now in seasons of dismay
  What cheering hope from thoughts of thee !
And how will earnest fancy stray
  To find its home where thou mayst be !

Sometimes I dream thee leaning o'er
  The harp I used to love so well ;
Again I tremble and adore
  The soul of its delicious swell ;
Again the very air is dim
  With eddies of harmonious might,
And all my brain and senses swim
  In a keen madness of delight.

Sometimes thy pensive form is seen
  On the dear seat beside the fire ;
There plainest thou with Madeline
  Or Isabella's lone desire.
He knows thee not, who does not know
  The tender flashing of thine eye
At some melodious tale of woe,
  And the sweet smile and sweeter sigh.

How oft in silent moonlight air,
  When the wide earth is full of rest,
And all things outward seem more fair
  For the inward spirit less opprest,
I look for thee, I think thee near,
  Thy tones are thrilling through my soul,
Thy dark eyes close to mine appear,
  And I am blest beyond control !

TO THE LOVED ONE

Yet deem not thou my absent state
  Is measured all by amorous moan;
Clear-voiced Love hath learned of Fate
  New harmonies of deeper tone.
All thoughts that in me live and burn,
  The thirst for truth, the sense of power;
Freedom's high hope—to thee they turn;
  I bring them as a precious dower!

The beauty which those thoughts adore
  Diffused through this perennial frame
Centres in thee; I feel it more
  Since thy delivering presence came:
And with a clearer affluence now
  That mystic spirit fills my heart,
Wafts me on hope's enthusiast flow,
  And heals with prayer the guilty smart.

Oh! best beloved, it were a bliss
  As pure as aught the angels feel,
To think in after days of this,
  Should time a strength in me reveal
To fill with worthy thoughts and deed
  The measure of my high desire;
To thee were due the glorious meed,
  Thy smile had kindled first the fire.

But if the starry courses give
  No eminence of light to me,
At least together we may live,
  Together loved and loving be;

At least what good my spirit knows
  Shall seek in thee a second birth,
And in thy gentle soul's repose
  I'll wean me from the things of earth.

Even now begins that holy life,
  For when I kneel in Christian prayer,
Thy name, my own, my promised wife,
  Is blent with mine in fondest care.
Oh pray for me that both may know
  That inward bridal's high delight,
And both beyond the grave may go
  Together in the Father's sight.

Jan. 1831.

TO MY MOTHER

WHEN barren doubt like a late coming snow
  Made an unkind December of my spring,
  That all the pretty flowers did droop for woe,
  And the sweet birds their love no more would
      sing:
Then the remembrance of thy gentle faith,
  Mother beloved, would steal upon my heart;
  Fond feeling saved me from that utter scathe,
  And from thy hope I could not live apart.
Now that my mind hath passed from wintry
      gloom,
  And on the calmèd waters once again
  Ascendant Faith circles with silver plume,
That casts a charmèd shade, not now in pain,
  Thou child of Christ, in joy I think of thee,
  And mingle prayers for what we both may be.

Jan. 1831.

A LOVER'S REPROOF

When two complaining spirits mingle,
  Saintly and calm their woes become :
Alas the grief that bideth single,
  Whose heart is drear, whose lips are dumb !
My drooping lily, when the tears
  Of morning bow thy tender head,
Oh scatter them, and have no fears :
  They kill sometimes if cherishèd,
Dear girl, the precious gift you gave
  Was of *yourself* entire and free.
Why front *alone* Life's gloomy wave,
  Why fling the brilliant foam to me ?
Am I the lover of thy mirth,
  A trifling thing of sunny days,—
A soul forbid for want of worth,
  To tread with thee th' unpleasant ways ?
No—trust me, love ; if I delight
  To mark thy brighter hour of pleasure,
To deep-eyed Passion's watchful sight
  Thy sadness is a costlier treasure.

July, 1831.

SONNET

A MELANCHOLY thought had laid me low;
A thought of self-desertion, and the death
Of feelings wont with my heart's blood to flow,
And feed the inner soul with purest breath.
The idle busy star of daily life,
Base passions, haughty doubts, and selfish fears,
Have withered up my being in a strife
Unkind, and dried the source of human tears.
One evening I went forth, and stood alone
With Nature: moon there was not, nor the light
Of any star in heaven: yet from the sight
Of that dim nightfall better hope hath grown
Upon my spirit, and from those cedars high
Solemnly changeless, as the very sky.

Sept. 1830.

A SCENE IN SUMMER

ALFRED, I would that you beheld me now,
Sitting beneath a mossy ivied wall
On a quaint bench, which to that structure old
Winds an accordant curve. Above my head
Dilates immeasurable a wild of leaves,
Seeming received into the blue expanse
That vaults this summer noon: before me lies
A lawn of English verdure, smooth and bright,
Mottled with fainter hues of early hay,
Whose fragrance, blended with the rose perfume
From that white flowering bush, invites my sense
To a delicious madness—and faint thoughts
Of childish years are borne into my brain
By unforgotten ardours waking now.
Beyond, a gentle slope leads into shade
Of mighty trees, to bend whose eminent crown
Is the prime labour of the pettish winds,
That now in lighter mood are twirling leaves
Over my feet, or hurrying butterflies,
And the gay humming things that summer loves,
Thro' the warm air, or altering the bound
Where yon elm shadows in majestic line
Divide dominion with the abundant light.

June, 1831.

SONNET

OH Poetry, oh rarest spirit of all
  That dwell within the compass of the mind,
  Forsake not him, whom thou of old didst call :
  Still let me seek thy face, and seeking find.
Some years have gone about since I and thou
  Became acquainted first : we met in woe ;
  Sad was my cry for help as it is now ;
  Sad too thy breathed response of music slow ;
But in that sadness was such essence fine,
  So keen a sense of Life's mysterious name,
  And high conceit of Natures more divine,
That breath and sorrow seemed no more the same.
  Oh let me hear again that sweet reply !
  More than by loss of thee I cannot die.

June, 1831.

SONNET

ALAS! that sometimes even a duteous life,
  If uninspired by love, and love-born joy,
  Grows fevered in the world's unholy strife,
  And sinks destroyed by that it would destroy!
Beloved, from the boisterous deeds that fill
  The measure up of this unquiet time,
  The dull monotonies of Faction's chime,
  And irrepressible thoughts foreboding ill,
I turn to thee as to a heaven apart—
  Oh! not apart, not distant, near me ever,
  So near my soul that nothing can thee sever!
How shall I fear, knowing there is for me
  A City of refuge, builded pleasantly
  Within the silent places of the heart?

May, 1831.

SONNET

WHY throbbest thou, my heart, why thickly breathest?
I ask no rich and splendid eloquence:
A few words of the warmest and the sweetest
Sure thou mayst yield without such coy pretence:
Open the chamber where affection's voice,
For rare occasions is kept close and fine:
Bid it but say, 'Sweet Emily, be mine,'
So for one boldness thou shalt aye rejoice.
Fain would I speak when the full music-streams
Rise from her lips to linger on her face,
Or like a form floating through Raffaelle's dreams,
Then fixed by him in ever living grace,
She sits i' the silent worship of mine eyes.
Courage, my heart: change thou for words thy sighs.

SONNET

STILL here—thou hast not faded from my sight,
  Nor all the music round thee from mine ear :
  Still grace flows from thee to the brightening
    year,
  And all the birds laugh out in wealthier light.
Still am I free to close my happy eyes,
  And paint upon the gloom thy mimic form,
  That soft white neck, that cheek in beauty
    warm,
  And brow half hidden where yon ringlet lies ;
With, oh ! the blissful knowledge all the while
  That I can lift at will each curvèd lid,
  And my fair dream most highly realise.
The time will come, 'tis ushered by my sighs,
  When I may shape the dark, but vainly bid
  True light restore that form, those looks, that
    smile.

SONNET

LADY, I bid thee to a sunny dome
  Ringing with echoes of Italian song ;
  Henceforth to thee these magic halls belong,
  And all the pleasant place is like a home.
Hark, on the right with full piano tone,
  Old Dante's voice encircles all the air ;
  Hark yet again, like flute-tones mingling rare,
  Comes the keen sweetness of Petrarca's moan.
Pass thou the lintel freely : without fear
  Feast on the music : I do better know thee,
  Than to suspect this pleasure thou dost owe me
Will wrong thy gentle spirit, or make less dear
  That element whence thou must draw thy life ;—
  An English maiden and an English wife.

SONNET

SPEED ye, warm hours, along th' appointed path,
Speed, though ye bring but pain, slow pain to me;
I will not much bemoan your heavy wrath,
So ye will make my lady glad and free.
What is 't that I must here confinèd be,
If she may roam the summer's sweets among,
See the full-cupped flower, the laden tree,
Hear from deep groves the thousand-voicèd song?
Sometimes in that still chamber will she sit
Trim ranged with books, and cool with dusky blinds,
That keep the moon out, there, as seemèd fit,
To sing, or play, or read—what sweet hope finds
Way to my heart? perchance some verse of mine—
Oh happy I! speed on, ye hours divine!

SONNET

WHEN gentle fingers cease to touch the string,
  Dear Charles, no music lingers on the lyre ;
  But the sea-shells from everlasting ring
  With the deep murmurs of their home desire :
Lean o'er the shell, and 'twill be heard to plain,
  Now low, now high, till all thy sense is gone
  Into the sweetness ; then depart again,
  Still though unheard, flows on that inner moan ;
Full oft like one of these our human heart
  Secretly murmurs on a loving lay,
  Though not a tone finds any outward way.
Then trust me, Charles, nor let it cause thee smart,
  That seldom in my songs thy name is seen—
  When most I loved, I most have silent been.

1831.

SONNET

THE garden trees are busy with the shower
  That fell ere sunset ; now methinks they talk,
  Lowly and sweetly as befits the hour,
  One to another down the grassy walk.
Hark the laburnum from his opening flower
  This cherry-creeper greets in whisper light,
  While the grim fir, rejoicing in the night,
  Hoarse mutters to the murmuring sycamore.
What shall I deem their converse? would they hail
  The wild grey light that fronts yon massive cloud,
  Or the half bow, rising like pillared fire?
Or are they sighing faintly for desire
  That with May dawn their leaves may be o'erflowed,
  And dews about their feet may never fail?

1831.

SCENE AT ROME

RAFAEL *sitting in his Studio*; FIAMMETTA *enters.*

R. Dearest, I wished for thee a moment gone,
And lo, upon the wish thou art here.
F. Perhaps
It was thy wish that even now as I entered,
Gleamed through the citron shadow, like a star-beam,
One starbeam of some high predominant star.
R. Why, little trifler, whither hast thou been
That thou return'st so fair fantastical?
F. Down by the fountain, where the dark cool alley
Yields into sudden light of cooler spray.
It is a noble evening—one to shame thee—
For the least hue of that all-coloured heaven
Bears a more full and rich divinity
Than the best touch thy pencil ever gave,—
Thou smilest at me.

R. Rather should I sigh
To think that while I learn to love thee better,
And better prize all that belongs to thee,
In the fair company I live with always,
The tempting faces, and warm loving shapes
That make my little room a paradise,
Thou wandering about, from lighted fountains,
From groves at twilight full of changing magic,
Or yon great gallery picture hung with stars,
Gatherest contempt for that poor mimic thing,
An artist.
F. Thou believest not thy words,
Else could I call a thousand witnesses
To swear me into innocence again.
R. Where are they?
F. Out alas! I had forgot—
I have them not—I know not where they dwell;
They roam in a dim field I may not come to,
Nor ever see them more; yet were they once
Familiar beings, inward to my soul
As is the lifeblood to the life.
R. The answer—
We have the riddle. Who are these unkind ones
Who knew the thing it is to be beside thee,
Looked on thy face, yet had the hearts to leave thee?
F. Oh there you are mistaken—you are too quick—
They had no eyes and could not see my face—

They had no power to stay—they must have
left me—
Each in his turn stood on the downcleft edge
Of a most mighty river, stood and fell,
Borne to the silent things that are no more.
R. Are they then dead?
F. Ay, dead; entombed within
A glorious sepulchre, to whose broad space
The world of present things is but an atom.
There they lie dead, and here I'd weep for
them,
But that I have a fairy mirror by me
Shows me their spirits, pale and beautiful
With a sweet mournful beauty.
R. Thou art mocking me;
These are but fancies thou art speaking of,
The incorporeal children of the brain.
F. Aha, brave Œdipus! my lady Sphinx
Had stood in danger with thee. Hast thou
guessed it?
These friends once harboured with me, now
departed,
These witnesses to my clear faith and fondness,
They are all Thoughts, all glorious thoughts of
thee,
Infinite in their number, bright as rainbows,
And in pervading presence visitant
Whenever I am forced to be alone,
And losing thee to talk with stars and streams.
R. And, by our Lady, 'tis a good exchange.

The stars and streams are silent—cannot chide
thee—
Will let a foolish woman talk by the hour
Her gentle nonsense, and reprove her never,
Nor with one frown dim their ambrosial smiles;
Thou find'st not me so easy.
F. Still suspicious!
What, must I tell thee all this day's employment;
Tell how I read the heavens with curious
glances,
And by a sort of wild astrology
Taught me by a young god, whose name is Love,
But who before all things resembles thee,
I tried to shape in those high starry eyes
The very looks of thine?
R. Nay, own Fiammetta,
If we must needs have such usurping spirits,
And turn the bright heavens from the things
they are
Into poor semblances of earthly creatures,
They shall be all thine own—take them and
wear them;
Be thou the moon, the sunset, that thou wilt
So I behold thee.
F. I will be the sky!
No narrower bound than its far unknown limit
Shall keep me prisoner. Thou hast called me
fair—
Often and often on my lips thou hast sworn it—

What wilt thou say when thou shalt see me come
To press thee in those blue celestial folds,
To gaze upon thee with a million eyes,
Each eye like these, and each a fire of love?
R. I would not have thee other than thou art,
Even in the least complexion of a dimple,
For all the pictures Pietro Perugin,
My master, ever painted. And pardon me,
I would not have the heavens anything
But what they are and were and still shall be,
Despite thy wish, Fiammetta. 'Tis not well
To make the eternal Beauty ministrant
To our frail lives and frailer human loves.
Three thousand years perhaps before we lived,
Some Eastern maiden framed thy very wish,
And loved and died, and in the passionless void
Vanished for ever. Yet this glorious Nature
Took not a thought of her, but shone above
The blank she left, as on the place she filled.
So will it be with us—a dark night waits us—
Another moment, we must plunge within it—
Let us not mar the glimpses of pure Beauty,
Now streaming in like moonlight, with the fears,
The joys, the hurried thoughts, that rise and fall
To the hot pulses of a mortal heart.
F. How now? Thy voice was wont to speak of Love:

I shall not know it, if its language change:
The clear, low utterance, and angelic tone
Will lose their music, if they praise not love.
R. And when I praise it not, or cease to fold thee
Thus in my arms, Fiammetta, may I die
Unwept, unhonoured, barred without the gate
Of that high temple, where I minister
With daily ritual of coloured lights
For candelabras, and pure saintly forms
To image forth the loveliness I serve.
I did but chide thee that thou minglest ever
Beauty with beauty, as with perfume perfume:
Thou canst not love a rosebud for itself,
But thinkest straight who gave that rose to thee;
The leaping fountain minds thee of the music
We heard together; and the very heaven,
The illimitable firmament of God,
Must steal a likeness to a Roman studio
Ere it can please thee.
F. I am a poor woman, Sir;
A woman, poor in all things but her heart,
And when I cease to love I cease to live.
You will not cure me of this heresy;
Flames would not burn it out, nor sharp rocks tear it.
R. I am a merciful Inquisitor;
I shall enjoin thee but a gentle penance.
F. The culprit trusts the judge, and feels no fear

In his immediate presence ; a rare thing
In Italy !—Proceed.
R. There was a thing
Thou askedst me this morning.
F. I remember—
To see the picture thou hast kept from me.
I prithee, let me.
R. It shall be thy penance
To find it full of faults, and not one beauty.
F. Where stands it ?
R. There, behind the canopy.
A great Venetian nobleman, esteemed
For a good judge, they say, by Lionardo,
Paid me a princely sum but yesterday
For this poor portrait.
F. Portrait ? and of whom ?
Is it a lady ?
R. Yes—a Roman lady—
About your stature ; and her hair is bound
With a pearl fillet, even as your own.
Her eyes are just Fiammetta's ; they are turned
On a fair youth, who sits beside her, gazing
As he would drink up all their light in his.
Upon her arm a bracelet ; and thereon
Is graven—
F. Name it !
R. RAPHAEL URBINENSIS.
F. This kiss—and this—reward thee. Let me see it.

1832.

ON SOME OF THE CHARACTERISTICS OF MODERN POETRY, AND ON THE LYRICAL POEMS OF ALFRED TENNYSON.

SO Mr. Montgomery's *Oxford*, by the help of some pretty illustrations, has contrived to prolong its miserable existence to a second edition! But this is slow work, compared to that triumphant progress of the *Omnipresence*, which, we concede to the author's friends, was 'truly astonishing.' We understand, moreover, that a new light has broken upon this 'desolator desolate;' and since the 'columns' have begun to follow the example of 'men and gods,' by whom our poetaster has long been condemned, 'it is the fate of genius,' he begins to discover, 'to be unpopular.' Now, strongly as we protest against Mr. Montgomery's application of this maxim to his own case, we are much disposed to agree with him as to its abstract correctness. Indeed, the truth which it involves seems to afford the only solution of so curious a phenomenon as the success, partial and transient though it be, of himself, and others of his calibre. When Mr. Wordsworth, in his celebrated Preface to the *Lyrical Ballads*, asserted that immediate or rapid popularity was not the test of poetry, great was the consternation and clamour among those farmers of public favour, the established critics. Never had so audacious an attack been made upon their undoubted privileges and hereditary charter of oppression. 'What! *The Edinburgh Review* not infallible!' shrieked the amiable petulance of Mr. Jeffrey. '*The Gentleman's Magazine* incapable of decision!' faltered the feeble garrulity of Silvanus Urban. And straightway the whole sciolist herd, men of rank, men of letters, men of wealth, men of business, all the 'mob of gentlemen who think with ease,' and a terrible number of old ladies and boarding-school misses began to scream in chorus, and prolonged the notes of execration with which they overwhelmed the new doctrine, until their wits and their voices fairly gave in from exhaustion. Much, no doubt, they did, for much persons will do when they fight for their dear selves: but there was one thing they could not do, and unfortunately it was the only one of any importance. They could not put down Mr. Wordsworth by clamour, or prevent his doctrine, once uttered, and enforced by his example, from awakening the minds of men, and giving a fresh impulse to art. It was the truth, and it prevailed; not only against the exasperation of that hydra, the Reading Public, whose vanity was hurt, and the blustering of its keepers, whose delusion was exposed, but even against the false glosses and narrow apprehensions of the Wordsworthians themselves. It is the madness of all who loosen some great principle, long buried under a snow-heap of custom and superstition, to imagine that they can restrain its operation, or circumscribe it by their purposes. But the right of private judgment was stronger than the will of Luther; and even the genius of Wordsworth cannot expand itself to the full periphery of poetic art.

It is not true, as his exclusive admirers would have it, that the highest species of poetry is the reflective: it is a gross fallacy, that, because certain opinions are acute or profound, the expression of them by the imagination must be eminently beautiful. Whenever the mind of the artist suffers itself to be occupied, during its periods of creation, by any other predominant motive than the desire of beauty, the result is false in art. Now there is undoubtedly no reason, why he may not find beauty in those moods of emotion, which arise from the combinations of reflective thought, and it is possible that he may delineate these with fidelity, and not be led astray by any suggestions of an unpoetical mood. But, though possible, it is hardly probable: for a man, whose reveries take a reasoning turn, and who is accustomed to measure his ideas by their logical relations rather than the congruity of the sentiments to which they refer, will be apt to mistake the pleasure he has in knowing a thing to be true, for the pleasure he would have in knowing it to be beautiful, and so will pile his thoughts in a rhetorical battery, that they may convince, instead of letting them glow in the natural course of contemplation, that they may enrapture. It would not be difficult to show, by reference to the most admired poems of Wordsworth, that he is frequently chargeable with this error, and that much has been said by him which is good as philosophy, powerful as rhetoric, but false as poetry. Perhaps this very distortion of the truth did more in the peculiar juncture of our literary affairs to enlarge and liberalise the genius of our age, than could have been effected by a less sectarian temper. However this may be, a new school of reformers soon began to attract attention, who, professing the same independence of immediate favour, took their stand on a different region of Parnassus from that occupied by the Lakers,* and one, in our opinion, much less liable to perturbing currents of air from ungenial climates. We shall not hesitate to express our conviction, that the Cockney school (as it was termed in derision, from a cursory view of its accidental circumstances) contained more genuine inspiration, and adhered more speedily to that portion of truth which it embraced, than any *form* of art that has existed in this country since the day of Milton. Their *caposetta* was Mr. Leigh Hunt, who did little more than point the way, and was diverted from his aim by a thousand personal predilections and political habits of thought. But he was followed by

* This cant term was justly ridiculed by Mr. Wordsworth's supporters; but it was not so easy to substitute an inoffensive denomination. We are not at all events the first who have used it without a contemptuous intention, for we remember to have heard a disciple quote Aristophanes in its behalf. *Οὗτος οὐ τῶν ἠθάδων τῶνδ' ὧν ὁρᾶθ' ὑμεῖς ἀεὶ, ἀλλὰ* ΛΙΜΝΑΙΟΣ. 'This is no common, no barn-door fowl: No, but a *Lakist*!'

two men of a very superior make ; men who were born poets, lived poets, and went poets to their untimely graves. Shelley and Keats were, indeed, of opposite genius ; that of the one was vast, impetuous, and sublime : the other seemed to be 'fed with honey-dew,' and to have 'drunk the milk of Paradise.' Even the softness of Shelley comes out in bold, rapid, comprehensive strokes ; he has no patience for minute beauties, unless they can be massed into a general effect of grandeur. On the other hand, the tenderness of Keats cannot sustain a lofty flight ; he does not generalise or allegorise Nature ; his imagination works with few symbols, and reposes willingly on what is given freely. Yet in this formal opposition of character there is, it seems to us, a ground-work of similarity sufficient for the purposes of classification, and constituting a remarkable point in the progress of literature. They are both poets of sensation rather than reflection. Susceptible of the slightest impulse from external nature, their fine organs trembled into emotion at colours, and sounds, and movements, unperceived, or unregarded by duller temperaments. Rich and clear were their perceptions of visible forms; full and deep their feelings of music. So vivid was the delight attending the simple exertions of eye and ear, that it became mingled more and more with their trains of active thought, and tended to absorb their whole being into the energy of sense. Other poets *seek* for images to illustrate their conceptions; these men had no need to seek; they lived in a world of images; for the most important and extensive portion of their life consisted in those emotions, which are immediately conversant with sensation. Like the hero of Goethe's novel, they would hardly have been affected by what are called the pathetic parts of a book; but the *merely beautiful* passages, 'those from which the spirit of the author looks clearly and mildly forth,' would have melted them to tears. Hence they are not descriptive; they are picturesque. They are not smooth and *negatively* harmonious; they are full of deep and varied melodies. This powerful tendency of imagination to a life of immediate sympathy with the external universe, is not nearly so liable to false views of art as the opposite disposition of purely intellectual contemplation. For where beauty is constantly passing before 'that inward eye, which is the bliss of solitude;' where the soul seeks it as a perpetual and necessary refreshment to the sources of activity and intuition; where all the other sacred ideas of our nature, the idea of good, the idea of perfection, the idea of truth, are habitually contemplated through the medium of this predominant mood, so that they assume its colour, and are subject to its peculiar laws—there is little danger that the ruling passion of the whole mind will cease to direct its creative operations, or the energetic principle of love for the beautiful sink, even for a brief period, to the level of a mere notion in the understanding. We do not deny that it is, on other accounts, dangerous for frail humanity to linger with fond attachment in the vicinity of sense. Minds of this description are especially liable to moral temptations, and upon them, more than any, it is incumbent to remember that their mission as men, which they share with all their fellow-beings, is of infinitely higher interest than their mission as artists, which they possess by rare and exclusive privilege. But it is obvious that, critically speaking, such temptations are of slight moment. Not the gross and evident passions of our nature, but the elevated and less separable desires are the dangerous enemies which misguide the poetic spirit in its attempts at self-cultivation. That delicate sense of fitness, which grows with the growth of artist feelings, and strengthens with their strength, until it acquires a celerity and weight of decision hardly inferior to the correspondent judgments of conscience, is weakened by every indulgence of heterogeneous aspirations, however pure they may be, however lofty, however suitable to human nature. We are therefore decidedly of opinion that the heights and depths of art are most within the reach of those who have received from Nature the 'fearful and wonderful' constitution we have described, whose poetry is a sort of magic, producing a number of impressions too multiplied, too minute, and too diversified to allow of our tracing them to their causes, because just such was the effect, even so boundless, and so bewildering, produced on their imaginations by the real appearance of Nature. These things being so, our friends of the new school had evidently much reason to recur to the maxim laid down by Mr. Wordsworth, and to appeal from the immediate judgments of lettered or unlettered contemporaries to the decision of a more equitable posterity. How should they be popular, whose senses told them a richer and ampler tale than most men could understand, and who constantly expressed, because they constantly felt, sentiments of exquisite pleasure or pain, which most men were not permitted to experience? The public very naturally derided them as visionaries, and gibbeted *in terrorem* those inaccuracies of diction, occasioned sometimes by the speed of their conceptions, sometimes by the inadequacy of language to their peculiar conditions of thought. But, it may be asked, does not this line of argument prove too much? Does it not prove that there is a barrier between these poets and all other persons, so strong and immovable, that, as has been said of the Supreme Essence, we must be themselves before we can understand them in the least? Not only are they not liable to sudden and vulgar estimation, but the lapse of ages, it seems, will not consolidate their fame, nor the suffrages of the wise few produce any impression, however remote or slowly matured, on the judgments of the incapacitated many. We answer, This is not the import of our argument. Undoubtedly the true poet addresses himself, in all his conceptions, to the common nature of us all. Art is a lofty tree, and may shoot up far beyond our grasp, but its roots are in daily life and experience.

Every bosom contains the elements of those complex emotions which the artist feels, and every head can, to a certain extent, go over in itself the process of their combination, so as to understand his expressions and sympathise with his state. But this requires exertion; more or less, indeed, according to the difference of occasion, but always some degree of exertion. For since the emotions of the poet, during composition, follow a regular law of association, it follows that to accompany their progress up to the harmonious prospect of the whole, and to perceive the proper dependence of every step on that which preceded, it is absolutely necessary *to start from the same point*, i.e. clearly to apprehend that leading sentiment in the poet's mind, by their conformity to which the host of suggestions is arranged. Now this requisite exertion is not willingly made by the large majority of readers. It is so easy to judge capriciously, and according to indolent impulse! For very many, therefore, it has become *morally* impossible to attain the author's point of vision, on account of their habits, or their prejudices, or their circumstances; but it is never *physically* impossible, because Nature has placed in every man the simple elements, of which art is the sublimation. Since then this demand on the reader for activity, when he wants to peruse his author in a luxurious passiveness, is the very thing that moves his bile, it is obvious that those writers will be always most popular, who require the least degree of exertion. Hence, whatever is mixed up with art, and appears under its semblance, is always more favourably regarded than art free and unalloyed. Hence, half the fashionable poems in the world are mere rhetoric, and half the remainder are perhaps not liked by the generality for their substantial merits. Hence, likewise, of the really pure compositions those are most universally agreeable, which take for their primary subject the *usual* passions of the heart, and deal with them in a simple state, without applying the transforming powers of high imagination. Love, friendship, ambition, religion, etc., are matters of daily experience, even amongst imaginative tempers. The forces of association, therefore, are ready to work in these directions, and little effort of will is necessary to follow the artist. For the same reason such subjects often excite a partial power of composition, which is no sign of a truly poetic organisation. We are very far from wishing to depreciate this class of poems, whose influence is so extensive, and communicates so refined a pleasure. We contend only that the facility with which its impressions are communicated, is no proof of its elevation as a form of art, but rather the contrary. What then, some may be ready to exclaim, is the pleasure derived by most men from Shakespeare, or Dante, or Homer, entirely false and factitious? If these are really masters of their art, must not the energy required of the ordinary intelligences, that come in contact with their mighty genius, be the greatest possible? How comes it then that they are popular?

Shall we not say, after all, that the difference is in the power of the author, not in the tenor of his meditations? Those eminent spirits find no difficulty in conveying to common apprehension their lofty sense, and profound observation of Nature. They keep no aristocratic state, apart from the sentiments of society at large; they speak to the hearts of all, and by the magnetic force of their conceptions elevate inferior intellects into a higher and purer atmosphere. The truth contained in this objection is undoubtedly important; geniuses of the most universal order, and assigned by destiny to the most propitious eras of a nation's literary development, have a clearer and larger access to the minds of their compatriots, than can ever be open to those who are circumscribed by less fortunate circumstances. In the youthful periods of any literature there is an expansive and communicative tendency in mind, which produces unreservedness of communion, and reciprocity of vigour between different orders of intelligence. Without abandoning the ground which has always been defended by the partisans of Mr. Wordsworth, who declare with perfect truth that the number of real admirers of what is really admirable in Shakespeare and Milton are much fewer than the number of apparent admirers might lead one to imagine, we may safely assert that the intense thoughts set in circulation by those 'orbs of song,' and their noble satellites, 'in great Eliza's golden time,' did not fail to awaken a proportionable intensity in the natures of numberless auditors. Some might feel feebly, some strongly; the effect would vary according to the character of the recipient; but upon none was the stirring influence entirely unimpressive. The knowledge and power thus imbibed, became a part of national existence; it was ours as Englishmen; and amid the flux of generations and customs we retain unimpaired this privilege of intercourse with greatness. But the age in which we live comes late in our national progress. That first raciness, and juvenile vigour of literature, when nature 'wantoned as in her prime, and played at will her virgin fancies,' is gone, never to return. Since that day we have undergone a period of degradation. 'Every handicraftsman has worn the mark of Poesy.' It would be tedious to repeat the tale, so often related, of French contagion, and the heresies of the Popian school. With the close of the last century came an era of reaction, an era of painful struggle, to bring our over-civilised condition of thought into union with the fresh productive spirit that brightened the morning of our literature. But repentance is unlike innocence: the laborious endeavour to restore has more complicated methods of action than the freedom of untainted nature. Those different powers of poetic disposition, the energies of Sensitive,* of Reflective, of

* We are aware that this is not the right word, being appropriated by common use to a different signification. Those who think the caution given by Caesar should not stand in the way of urgent occasion, may substitute 'sensuous,' a word in use amongst our elder divines, and revived by a few bold writers in our own time.

Passionate Emotion, which in former times were intermingled, and derived from mutual support an extensive empire over the feelings of men, were now restrained within separate spheres of agency. The whole system no longer worked harmoniously, and by intrinsic harmony acquired external freedom; but there arose a violent and unusual action in the several component functions, each for itself, all striving to reproduce the regular power which the whole had once enjoyed. Hence the melancholy, which so evidently characterises the spirit of modern poetry; hence that return of the mind upon itself, and the habit of seeking relief in idiosyncrasies rather than community of interest. In the old times the poetic impulse went along with the general impulse of the nation; in these, it is a reaction against it, a check acting for conservation against a propulsion towards change. We have indeed seen it urged in some of our fashionable publications, that the diffusion of poetry must necessarily be in the direct ratio of the diffusion of machinery, because a highly civilised people must have new objects of interest, and thus a new field will be opened to description. But this notable argument forgets that against this *objective* amelioration may be set the decrease of *subjective* power, arising from a prevalence of social activity, and a continual absorption of the higher feelings into the palpable interests of ordinary life. The French Revolution may be a finer theme than the war of Troy; but it does not so evidently follow that Homer is to find his superior. Our inference, therefore, from this change in the relative position of artists to the rest of the community is, that modern poetry, in proportion to its depth and truth, is likely to have little immediate authority over public opinion. Admirers it will have; sects consequently it will form; and these strong under-currents will in time sensibly affect the principal stream. Those writers, whose genius, though great, is not strictly and essentially poetic, become mediators between the votaries of art and the careless cravers for excitement.* Art herself, less manifestly glorious than in her periods of undisputed supremacy, retains her essential prerogatives, and forgets not to raise up chosen spirits, who may minister to her state, and vindicate her title.

One of this faithful Islâm, a poet in the truest and highest sense, we are anxious to present to our readers. He has yet written little, and published less; but in these 'preludes of a loftier strain,' we recognise the inspiring god. Mr. Tennyson belongs decidedly to the class we have already described as Poets of Sensation. He sees all the forms of nature with the *eruditus oculus*, and his ear has a fairy fineness. There is a strange earnestness in his worship of beauty, which throws a charm over his

* May we not compare them to the bright, but unsubstantial clouds which, in still evenings, girdle the sides of lofty mountains, and seem to form a natural connection between the lowly valleys, spread out beneath, and those isolated peaks above, that hold the 'last parley with the setting sun'?

impassioned song, more easily felt than described, and not to be escaped by those who have once felt it. We think he has more definiteness, and soundness of general conception, than the late Mr. Keats, and is much more free from blemishes of diction and hasty capriccios of fancy. He has also this advantage over that poet, and his friend Shelley, that he comes before the public, unconnected with any political party, or peculiar system of opinions. Nevertheless, true to the theory we have stated, we believe his participation in their characteristic excellencies is sufficient to secure him a share in their unpopularity. The volume of *Poems, chiefly Lyrical*, does not contain above 154 pages; but it shows us much more of the character of its parent mind than many books we have known of much larger compass, and more boastful pretensions. The features of original genius are clearly and strongly marked. The author imitates nobody; we recognise the spirit of his age, but not the individual form of this or that writer. His thoughts bear no more resemblance to Byron or Scott, Shelley or Coleridge, than to Homer or Calderon, Ferdusi or Calidas. We have remarked five distinctive excellencies of his own manner. First, his luxuriance of imagination, and at the same time his control over it. Secondly, his power of embodying himself in ideal characters, or rather moods of character, with such extreme accuracy of adjustment, that the circumstances of the narration seem to have a natural correspondence with the predominant feeling, and, as it were, to be evolved from it by assimilative force. Thirdly, his vivid, picturesque delineation of objects, and the peculiar skill with which he holds all of them *fused*, to borrow a metaphor from science, in a medium of strong emotion. Fourthly, the variety of his lyrical measures, and exquisite modulation of harmonious words and cadences to the swell and fall of the feelings expressed. Fifthly, the elevated habits of thought, *implied* in these compositions, and imparting a mellow soberness of tone, more impressive, to our minds, than if the author had drawn up a set of opinions in verse, and sought to instruct the understanding, rather than to communicate the love of beauty to the heart. We shall proceed to give our readers some specimens in illustration of these remarks, and, if possible, we will give them entire; for no poet can fairly be judged of by fragments, least of all a poet, like Mr. Tennyson, whose mind conceives nothing isolated, nothing abrupt, but every part with reference to some other part, and in subservience to the idea of the whole.

Recollections of the Arabian Nights!— What a delightful, endearing title! How we pity those to whom it calls up no reminiscence of early enjoyment, no sentiment of kindliness as towards one who sings a song they have loved, or mentions with affection a departed friend! But let nobody expect a multifarious enumeration of Viziers, Barmecides, Fire-worshippers, and Cadis; trees that sing, horses that fly, and Goules that eat rice-pudding! Our author knows what he is about: he has, with great judgment, selected our old acquaintance, 'the good Haroun Alraschid,' as the most prominent object of our childish interest, and with him has called up one of those luxurious garden scenes, the account of which, in plain prose, used to make our mouths water for sherbet, since luckily we were too young to think much about Zobeide! We think this poem will be the favourite among Mr. Tennyson's admirers; perhaps upon the whole it is our own; at least we find ourselves recurring to it oftener than to any other, and every time we read it, we feel the freshness of its beauty increase, and are inclined to exclaim with Madame de Sévigné, '*à force d'être ancien, il m'est nouveau.*' But let us draw the curtain.

1

When the breeze of a joyful dawn blew free
In the silken sail of infancy,
The tide of time flowed back with me,
The forward-flowing tide of time;
And many a sheeny summer-morn
Adown the Tigris I was borne,

By Bagdat's shrines of fretted gold,
High-walled gardens green and old;
  True Mussulman was I and sworn,
  For it was in the golden prime
  Of good Haroun Alraschid.

II

Anight my shallop, rustling through
The low and bloomed foliage, drove
The fragrant, glistening deeps, and clove
The citron-shadows in the blue;
By garden porches on the brim,
The costly doors flung open wide,
Gold glittering through lamplight dim,
And broidered sofas on each side:
  In sooth it was a goodly time,
  For it was in the golden prime
  Of good Haroun Alraschid.

III

Often, where clear-stemmed platans guard
The outlet, did I turn away
The boat-head down a broad canal
From the main river sluiced, where all
The sloping of the moonlit sward
Was damask work, and deep inlay
Of braided blossoms unmown, which crept
Adown to where the waters slept.
  A goodly place, a goodly time,
  For it was in the golden prime
  Of good Haroun Alraschid.

IV

A motion from the river won
Ridged the smooth level, bearing on
My shallop through the star-strown calm,
Until another night in night
I entered, from the clearer light,
Imbowered vaults of pillared palm,
Imprisoning sweets, which as they clomb
Heavenward, were stayed beneath the dome
  Of hollow boughs. A goodly time,
  For it was in the golden prime
  Of good Haroun Alraschid !

V

Still onward and the clear canal
Is rounded to as clear a lake.
From the green rivage many a fall
Of diamond rillets musical,
Through little crystal arches low,
Down from the central fountain's flow
Fall'n silver-chiming, seemed to shake
The sparkling flints beneath the prow.
  A goodly place, a goodly time,
  For it was in the golden prime
  Of good Haroun Alraschid !

VI

Above through many a bowery turn
A walk with vary-coloured shells
Wandered engrained. On either side,
All round about the fragrant marge,
From fluted vase and brazen urn

In order, eastern flowers large,
Some dropping low their crimson bells
Half closed, and others studded wide
  With dicks and diars, fed the time
  With odour in the golden prime
  Of good Haroun Alraschid!

VII

Far off and where the lemon grove
In closest coverture upsprang,
The living airs of middle night
Died round the Bulbul as he sang:
Not he; but something which possessed
The darkness of the world, delight,
Life, anguish, death, immortal love,
Ceasing not, mingled, unrepressed,
  Apart from place, withholding time,
  But flattering the golden prime
  Of good Haroun Alraschid.

VIII

Black-green the garden bowers and grots
Slumbered: the solemn palms were ranged
Above, unwooed of summer wind.
A sudden splendour from behind
Flushed all the leaves with rich gold-green,
And flowing rapidly between
Their interspaces, counterchanged
The level lake with diamond plots
  Of saffron light. A lovely time,
  For it was in the golden prime
  Of good Haroun Alraschid!

IX

Dark-blue the deep sphere overhead,
Distinct with vivid stars unrayed,
Grew darker from that underflame;
So leaping lightly from the boat,
With silver anchor left afloat,
In marvel whence that glory came
Upon me, as in sleep I sank
In cool, soft turf upon the bank,
  Entranced with that place and time,
  So worthy of the golden prime
  Of good Haroun Alraschid.

X

Thence through the garden I was borne;
A realm of pleasance; many a mound
And many a shadow-chequered lawn
Full of the city's stilly sound;
And deep myrrh thickets blowing round
The stately cedar, tamarisks,
Thick rosaries of scented thorn,
Tall orient shrubs, and obelisks
  Graven with emblems of the time,
  In honour of the golden prime
  Of good Haroun Alraschid.

XI

With dazèd vision unawares
From the long alley's latticed shade
Emerged, I came upon the great
Pavilion of the Caliphat.

Right to the carven cedarn doors,
Flung inward over spangled floors,
Broad-based flights of marbled stairs
Ran up with golden balustrade,
  After the fashion of the time,
  And humour of the golden prime
  Of good Haroun Alraschid.

XII

The fourscore windows all alight
As with the quintessence of flame,
A million tapers flaring bright
From wreathed silvers looked to shame
The hollow-vaulted dark, and streamed
Upon the moonèd domes aloof
In inmost Bagdat, till there seemed
Hundreds of crescents on the roof
  Of night new-risen, that marvellous time,
  To celebrate the golden prime
  Of good Haroun Alraschid.

XIII

Then stole I up, and trancedly
Gazed on the Persian girl alone,
Serene with argent-lidded eyes
Amorous, and lashes like to rays
Of darkness, and a brow of pearl
Tressed with redolent ebony,
In many a dark, delicious curl
Flowing below her rose-hued zone:
  The sweetest lady of the time,
  Well worthy of the golden prime
  Of good Haroun Alraschid.

XIV.

Six columns, three on either side,
Pure silver, underpropped a rich
Throne o' the massive ore, from which
Down-drooped, in many a floating fold,
Engarlanded and diapered
With inwrought flowers, a cloth of gold.
Thereon, his deep eye laughter-stirred
With merriment of kingly pride,
  Sole star of all that place and time,
  I saw him—in his golden prime,
  The good Haroun Alraschid!

Criticism will sound but poorly after this; yet we cannot give silent votes. The first stanza, we beg leave to observe, places us at once in the position of feeling, which the poem requires. The scene is before us, around us; we cannot mistake its localities, or blind ourselves to its colours. That happy ductility of childhood returns for the moment; 'true Mussulmans are we, and sworn,' and yet there is a latent knowledge, which heightens the pleasure, that to our change from really childish thought we owe the capacities by which we enjoy the recollection. As the poem proceeds, all is in perfect keeping. There is a solemn distinctness in every image, a majesty of slow motion in every cadence, that aids the illusion of thought, and steadies its contemplation of the complete picture. Originality of observation seems to cost nothing to our author's liberal genius; he lavishes images of exquisite accuracy and elaborate splendour, as a common writer throws about metaphorical truisms, and exhausted tropes. Amidst all the varied luxuriance of the sensations described, we are never permitted to lose sight of the idea which gives unity to this variety, and by the recurrence of which, as a sort of mysterious influence, at the close of every stanza, the mind is wrought up, with consummate art, to the final disclosure. This poem is a perfect gallery of pictures; and the concise boldness, with which in a few words an object is clearly painted, is sometimes (see the 6th stanza) majestic as Milton, sometimes (see the 12th) sublime as Æschylus. We have not, however, so far forgot our vocation as critics, that we would leave without notice the slight faults which adhere to this precious work. In the 8th stanza, we doubt the propriety of using the bold compound 'black-green,' at least in such close vicinity to 'gold-green': nor is it perfectly clear by the term, although indicated by the context, that 'diamond plots' relates to shape rather than colour. We are perhaps very stupid, but 'vivid stars unrayed' does not convey to us a very precise notion. '*Rosaries* of scented thorn,' in the 10th stanza, is, we believe, an entirely unauthorised use of the word. Would our author translate '*biferique rosaria Faesti*'—'And *rosaries* of Paestum, twice in bloom'? To the beautiful 13th stanza, we are sorry to find any objection; but even the bewitching loveliness of that 'Persian girl' shall not prevent our performing the rigid duty we have undertaken, and we must hint to Mr. Tennyson that 'redolent' is no synonym for 'fragrant.' Bees may be redolent *of* honey: spring may be 'redolent *of* youth and love,' but the absolute use of the word has, we fear, neither in Latin nor English, any better authority than the monastic epitaph on Fair Rosamond: '*Hic jacet in tombâ Rosa Mundi, non Rosa Munda, non redolet, sed olet, quae redolere solet.*'

We are disposed to agree with Mr. Coleridge, when he says 'no adequate compensation can be made for the mischief a writer does by confounding the distinct senses of words.' At the same time our feelings in this instance rebel strongly in behalf of 'redolent'; for the melody of the passage, as it stands, is beyond the possibility of improvement, and unless he should chance to light upon a word very nearly resembling this in consonants and vowels, we can hardly quarrel with Mr. Tennyson if, in spite of our judgment, he retains the offender in his service.

Our next specimen is of a totally different character, but not less complete, we think, in its kind. Have we among our readers any who delight in the heroic poems of Old England, the inimitable ballads? Any to whom *Sir Patrick Spens*, and *Clym of the Clough*, and *Glorious Robin*, are consecrated names? Any who sigh with disgust at the miserable abortions of simpleness mistaken for simplicity, or florid weakness substituted for plain energy, which they may often have seen dignified with the title of Modern Ballads? Let us draw near, and read *The Ballad of Oriana.* We know no more happy seizure of the antique spirit in the whole compass of our literature; yet there is no foolish self-desertion, no attempt at obliterating the present, but everywhere a full discrimination of how much ought to be yielded, and how much retained. The author is well aware that the art of one generation cannot *become* that of another by any will or skill: but the artist may transfer the spirit of the past, making it a temporary form for his own spirit, and so effect, by idealising power, a new and legitimate combination. If we were asked to name among the real antiques that which bears greatest resemblance to this gem, we should refer to the ballad of *Fair*

Helen of Kirkconnel Lea in the *Minstrelsy of the Scottish Border.* It is a resemblance of mood, not of execution. They are both highly wrought lyrical expressions of pathos; and it is very remarkable with what intuitive art, every expression and cadence in *Fair Helen* is accorded to the main feeling. The characters that distinguish the language of our *lyrical*, from that of our *epic* ballads, have never yet been examined with the accuracy they deserve. But, beyond question, the class of poems, which, in point of harmonious combination, *Oriana* most resembles, is the Italian. Just thus the meditative tenderness of Dante and Petrarch is embodied in the clear, searching tones of Tuscan song. These mighty masters produce two-thirds of their effect by *sound.* Not that they sacrifice sense to sound, but that sound conveys their meaning, where words would not. There are innumerable shades of fine emotion in the human heart, especially when the senses are keen and vigilant, which are too subtle and too rapid to admit of corresponding phrases. The understanding takes no definite note of them; how then can they leave signatures in language? Yet they exist; in plenitude of being and beauty they exist; and in music they find a medium through which they pass from heart to heart. The tone becomes the sign of the feeling; and they reciprocally suggest each other. Analogous to this suggestive power, may be reckoned, perhaps, in a sister art, the effects of Venetian colouring. Titian *explains* by tints, as Petrarch by tones. Words would not have done the business of the one, nor any groupings, or *narration by form*, that of the other. But, shame upon us! we are going back to our metaphysics, when that 'sweet, meek face' is waiting to be admitted.

I

My heart is wasted with my woe,
Oriana.
There is no rest for me below,
Oriana.

When the long dun wolds are ribbed with snow,
And loud the Norland whirlwinds blow,
Oriana,
Alone I wander to and fro,
Oriana.

II

Ere the light on dark was growing,
Oriana,
At midnight the cock was crowing,
Oriana :
Winds were blowing, waters flowing,
We heard the steeds to battle going,
Oriana :
Aloud the hollow bugle blowing,
Oriana.

III

In the yew-wood, black as night,
Oriana,
Ere I rode into the fight,
Oriana,
While blissful tears blinded my sight,
By starshine and by moonlight,
Oriana,
I to thee my troth did plight,
Oriana.

IV

She stood upon the castle wall,
Oriana :
She watched my crest among them all,
Oriana :

She saw me fight, she heard me call,
When forth there stepped a foeman tall,
Oriana,
Atween me and the castle wall,
Oriana.

V

The bitter arrow went aside,
Oriana :
The false, false arrow went aside,
Oriana :
The damn'd arrow glanced aside,
And pierced thy heart, my love, my bride,
Oriana !
Thy heart, my life, my love, my bride,
Oriana !

VI

Oh narrow, narrow was the space,
Oriana.
Loud, loud rang out the bugle's brays,
Oriana.
Oh, deathful stabs were dealt apace ;
The battle deepened in its place,
Oriana ;
But I was down upon my face,
Oriana.

VII

They should have stabbed me where I lay,
Oriana !
How could I rise and come away,
Oriana !

How could I look upon the day?
They should have stabbed me where I lay,
Oriana;
They should have trod me into clay,
Oriana!

VIII

Oh breaking heart that will not break,
Oriana;
Oh pale, pale face so sweet and meek,
Oriana;
Thou smilest, but thou dost not speak,
And then the tears run down thy cheek,
Oriana;
Whom wantest thou? whom dost thou seek,
Oriana?

IX

I cry aloud: none hears my cries,
Oriana.
Thou com'st atween me and the skies,
Oriana.
I feel the tears of blood arise
Up from my heart unto my eyes,
Oriana.
Within thy heart my arrow lies,
Oriana.

X

Oh cursed hand! oh cursed blow!
Oriana!
Oh happy thou that liest low,
Oriana!

All night the silence seems to flow
Beside me in my utter woe,
Oriana.
A weary, weary way I go,
Oriana.

XI

When Norland winds pipe down the lea,
Oriana,
I walk, I dare not think of thee,
Oriana.
Thou liest beneath the greenwood tree:
I dare not die, and come to thee,
Oriana—
I hear the roaring of the sea,
Oriana.

We have heard it objected to this poem that the name occurs once too often in every stanza. We have taken the plea into our judicial consideration, and the result is, that we overrule it, and pronounce that the proportion of the melodious cadences to the pathetic parts of the narration, could not be diminished without materially affecting the rich lyrical impression of the ballad. For what is the author's intention? To gratify our curiosity with a strange adventure? To shake our nerves with a painful story? Very far from it. Tears indeed may 'blind our sight,' as we read; but they are 'blissful tears': the strong musical delight prevails over every painful feeling, and mingles them all in its deep swell, until they attain a composure of exalted sorrow, a mood in which the latest repose of agitation becomes visible, and the influence of beauty spreads like light, over the surface of the mind. The last line, with its dreamy wildness, reveals the design of the whole. It is transferred, if we mistake not, from an old ballad (a freedom of immemorial usage with ballad-mongers, as our readers doubtless know), but the merit lies in the abrupt application of it to the leading sentiment, so as to flash upon us in a few little words a world of meaning, and to consecrate the passion that was beyond cure or hope, by resigning it to the accordance of inanimate Nature, who, like man, has her tempests, and occasions of horror, but august in their largeness of operation, awful by their dependence on a fixed and perpetual necessity.

We must give one more extract, and we are almost tempted to choose by lot among many that crowd on our recollection, and solicit our preference with such witchery as it is not easy to withstand. The poems towards the middle of the volume seem to have been written at an earlier period than the rest. They display more unrestrained fancy, and are less evidently proportioned to their ruling ideas, than those which we think of later date. Yet in the *Ode to Memory*—the only one which we have the poet's authority for referring to early life—there is a majesty of expression, united to a truth of thought, which almost confounds our preconceived distinctions. The '*Confessions of a Second-rate, Sensitive Mind*,' are full of deep insight into human nature, and into those particular trials, which are sure to beset men who think and feel for themselves at this epoch of social development. The title is perhaps ill-chosen: not only has it an appearance of quaintness, which has no sufficient reason, but it seems to us incorrect. The mood portrayed in this poem, unless the admirable skill of delineation has deceived us, is rather the clouded season of a strong mind, than the habitual condition of one feeble and 'second-rate.' Ordinary tempers build up fortresses of opinion on one side or another; they will see only what they choose to see; the distant glimpse of such an agony as is here brought out to view, is sufficient to keep them for ever in illusions, voluntarily raised at first, but soon trusted in with full reliance as inseparable parts of self. Perhaps, however, Mr. Tennyson's mode of 'rating' is different from ours. He may esteem none worthy of the first order, who has not attained a complete universality of thought, and such trustful reliance on a principle of repose, which lies beyond the war of conflicting opinions, that the grand ideas, '*qui planent sans cesse au dessus de l'humanité*,' cease to affect him with bewildering impulses of hope and fear. We have not space to enter further into this topic; but we should not despair of convincing Mr. Tennyson, that such a position of intellect would not be the most elevated, nor even the most conducive to perfection of art. The *How and the Why* appears to present the reverse of the same picture. It is the same mind still; the sensitive sceptic, whom we have looked upon in his hour of distress, now scoffing at his own state with an earnest mirth that borders on sorrow. It is exquisitely beautiful to see in this, as in the former portrait, how the feeling of art is kept ascendant in our minds over distressful realities, by constant reference to images of tranquil beauty, whether touched pathetically, as the Ox and the Lamb in the first piece, or with fine humour, as the 'great bird' and 'little bird' in the second. *The Sea Fairies* is another strange title; but those who turn to it with the very natural curiosity of discovering who these new births of mythology may be, will be unpardonable if they do not linger over it with higher feelings. A stretch of lyrical power is here exhibited, which we did not think the English language had possessed. The proud swell of verse, as the harp tones 'run up the ridged sea,' and the soft and melancholy lapse, as the sounds die along the widening space of waters, are instances of that right imitation which is becoming to art, but which in the hands of the unskilful, or the affecters of easy popularity, is often converted into a degrading mimicry, detrimental to the best interests of the imagination. A considerable portion of this book is taken up with a very singular, and very beautiful class of poems, on which the author has evidently bestowed much thought and elaboration. We allude to the female characters, every trait of which presumes an uncommon degree of observation and reflection. Mr. Tennyson's way of proceeding seems to be this. He collects the most striking phenomena of individual minds, until he arrives at some leading fact, which allows him to lay down an axiom or law, and then, working on the law thus attained, he clearly discerns the tendency of what new particulars his invention suggests, and is enabled to impress an individual freshness and unity on ideal combinations. These expressions of character are brief and coherent: nothing extraneous to the dominant fact is admitted, nothing illustrative of it, and, as it were, growing out of it, is rejected. They are like summaries of mighty dramas. We do not say this method admits of such large luxuriance of power as that of our real dramatists; but we contend that it is a new species of poetry, a graft of the lyric on the dramatic, and Mr. Tennyson deserves the laurel of an inventor, an enlarger of our modes of knowledge and power. We must hasten to make our election; so, passing by the 'airy, fairy Lilian,' who 'clasps her hands' in vain to retain us; the 'stately flower' of matronly fortitude, 'revered Isabel'; Madeline, with her voluptuous alternation of smile and frown; Mariana, last, but oh not least—we swear by the memory of

Shakespeare, to whom a monument of observant love has here been raised by simply expanding all the latent meanings and beauties contained in one stray thought of his genius—we shall fix on a lovely, albeit somewhat mysterious lady, who has fairly taken our 'heart from out our breast.'

ADELINE.

Mystery of mysteries,
Faintly smiling Adeline,
Scarce of earth, nor all divine,
Nor unhappy, nor at rest;
But beyond expression fair,
With thy floating flaxen hair,
Thy rose lips and full blue eyes
Take the heart from out my breast:
Wherefore those dim looks of thine,
Shadowy, dreaming Adeline?
Whence that aery bloom of thine,
Like a lily which the sun
Looks through in his sad decline,
And a rose-bush leans upon,
Thou that faintly smilest still
As a Naiad in a well,
Looking at the set of day,
Or a phantom, two hours old,
Of a maiden past away,
Ere the placid lips be cold?

Wherefore those faint smiles of thine,
Spiritual Adeline?
What hope or fear or joy is thine?
Who talketh with thee, Adeline,
For sure thou art not all alone?
Do beating hearts of salient springs
Keep measure with thine own?
Hast thou heard the butterflies,
What they say betwixt their wings?
Or in stillest evenings
With what voice the violet woos
To his heart the silver dews?
Or when little airs arise,
How the merry bluebell rings
To the mosses underneath?
Hast thou looked upon the breath
Of the lilies at sunrise?
Wherefore that faint smile of thine,
Shadowy dreaming Adeline?
Some honey-converse feeds thy mind
Some spirit of a crimson rose
In love with thee forgets to close
His curtains, wasting odorous sighs
All night long on darkness blind.
What aileth thee? whom waitest thou
With thy softened, shadowed brow,
And those dewlit eyes of thine,
Thou faint smiler, Adeline?
Lovest thou the doleful wind,
When thou gazest at the skies?
Doth the low-tongued Orient
Wander from the side o' the morn

Dripping with Sabæan spice
On thy pillow, lowly bent
With melodious airs lovelorn,
Breathing light against thy face,
While his locks a dropping twined
Round thy neck in subtle ring
Make a carcanet of rays,
And we talk together still
In the language, wherewith Spring
Letters cowslips on the hill?
Hence that look and smile of thine,
Spiritual Adeline.

Is not this beautiful? When this Poet dies, will not the Graces and the Loves mourn over him, '*fortunatâque favillâ nascentur violæ*'? How original is the imagery, and how delicate! How wonderful the new world thus created for us, the region between real and unreal! The gardens of Armida were but poorly musical compared with the roses and lilies that bloom around thee, thou faint smiler, Adeline, on whom the glory of imagination reposes, endowing all thou lookest on with sudden and mysterious life. We could expatiate on the deep meaning of this poem, but it is time to twitch our critical mantles; and, as our trade is not that of mere enthusiasm, we shall take our leave with an objection (perhaps a cavil) to the language of cowslips, which we think too ambiguously spoken of for a subject on which nobody, except Mr. Tennyson, can have any information. The 'ringing bluebell' too, if it be not a pun, suggests one, and might probably be altered to advantage.

One word more, before we have done, and it shall be a word of praise. The language of this book, with one or two rare exceptions, is thorough and sterling English. A little more respect, perhaps, was due to the '*jus et norma loquendi*,' but we are inclined to consider as venial a fault arising from generous enthusiasm for the principles of sound analogy, and for that Saxon element, which constitutes the intrinsic freedom and nervousness of our native tongue. We see no signs in what Mr. Tennyson has written of the Quixotic spirit which has led some persons to desire the reduction of English to a single form, by excluding nearly the whole of Latin and Roman derivatives. Ours is necessarily a compound language; as such alone it can flourish and increase; nor will the author of the poems we have extracted be likely to barter for a barren appearance of symmetrical structure that fertility of expression, and variety of harmony, which 'the speech, that Shakespeare spoke,' derived from the sources of southern phraseology.

In presenting this young poet to the public, as one not studious of instant popularity, nor likely to obtain it, we may be thought to play the part of a fashionable lady, who deludes her refractory mate into doing what she chooses, by pretending to wish the exact contrary, or of a cunning pedagogue, who practises a similar manœuvre on some self-willed Flibbertigibbet of the schoolroom. But the supposition would do us wrong. We have spoken in good faith, commending this volume to feeling hearts and imaginative tempers, not to the stupid readers, or the voracious readers, or the malignant readers, or the readers after dinner! We confess, indeed, we never knew an instance in which the theoretical abjurers of popularity have shown themselves very reluctant to admit its actual advances; so much virtue is not, perhaps, in human nature; and if the world should take a fancy to buy up these poems, in order to be revenged on the *Englishman's Magazine*, who knows whether even we might not disappoint its malice by a cheerful adaptation of our theory to 'existing circumstances'?

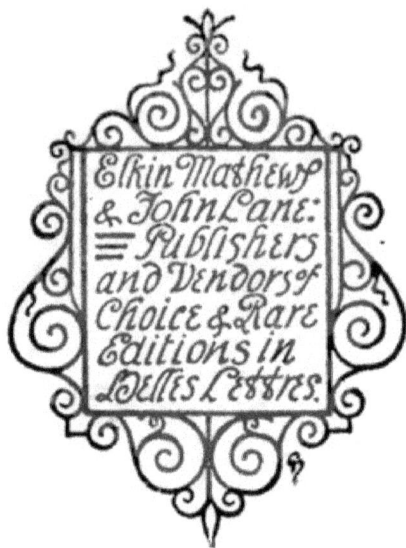

Elkin Mathews
& John Lane:
Publishers
and Vendors of
Choice & Rare
Editions in
Belles Lettres.

LONDON, VIGO STREET, W.
1893.

ELKIN MATHEWS & JOHN LANE'S

List of New and Forthcoming Books

WATSON (WILLIAM) THE ELOPING ANGELS: A CAPRICE. Title-page and Cover designed by WARRINGTON HOGG. Second Edition. Square 16mo, 3s. 6d. net, uniform with the Author's volume 'Epigrams.'

WATSON (WILLIAM) EXCURSIONS IN CRITICISM: being some Prose Recreations of a Rhymer. Second Edition. Crown 8vo, 5s. net.

WATSON (WILLIAM) THE PRINCE'S QUEST, AND OTHER POEMS. Second Edition. Fcap. 8vo, 4s. 6d. net.

*** Uniform with the Author's 'Poems.' (Macmillans.)

GALE (NORMAN) ORCHARD SONGS, 12mo, 5s. net.

WEDMORE (FREDERICK) RENUNCIATIONS. (A Chemis in the Suburbs—A Confidence at the Savile—The Nort Coast and Eleanor.) Post 8vo, 3s. 6d. net. [*All sold*

Also 50 copies L. P., 10s. 6d. net. [*A few remain*

WILDE (OSCAR) SALOMÉ: DRAME EN UN ACTE. Firs Edition limited to 600 copies (500 of which are for Sale for Paris and London. 8vo, 5s. net.

*** 'Salomé' has been accepted by Madame Bernhardt, but, as is we known, the Lord Chamberlain refused the licence.

NOBLE (J. ASHCROFT) THE SONNET IN ENGLAND, AN OTHER ESSAYS. Title-page and Cover designed by AUSTIN YOUNG. Small 8vo, 5s. net.

Also 50 copies L. P., Dickinson hand-made, 12s. 6d. net.

DAVIDSON (JOHN) FLEET STREET ECLOGUES. 300 copies, 12mo, buckram, 5s. net.

SYMONDS (JOHN ADDINGTON) IN THE KEY OF BLUE AND OTHER PROSE ESSAYS. With Cover (blue-bells and laurel) specially designed by C. S. RICKETTS. Second Edition. Crown 8vo, 8s. 6d. net.

NETTLESHIP (J. T.) ROBERT BROWNING: ESSAYS AND THOUGHTS. Third Edition. Crown 8vo, 5s. 6d.

SCOTT (WILLIAM BELL) A POET'S HARVEST HOME, with an AFTERMATH. Post 12mo, 5s. net.

HAZLITT (WILLIAM) LIBER AMORIS; OR, THE NEW PYGMALION. With an Introduction by RICHARD LE GALLIENNE. 12mo, 5s. net.

LE GALLIENNE (RICHARD) ENGLISH POEMS. Second Edition, 12mo, 5s. net.

LE GALLIENNE (RICHARD) GEORGE MEREDITH: SOME CHARACTERISTICS. With a Bibliography by JOHN LANE. Third Edition. Crown 8vo, 5s. 6d. net.

LE GALLIENNE (RICHARD) THE RELIGION OF A LITERARY MAN. 12mo, 3s. 6d. net; and a limited edition on hand-made paper, 10s. 6d. net.

MARTIN (W. WILSEY) QUATRAINS: LIFE'S MYSTERY, AND OTHER POEMS. 16mo, 2s. 6d. net.

HALLAM (ARTHUR) POEMS OF. Reprinted from the scarce 'Remains in Verse and Prose,' 1834. Also his critique from the 'Englishman's Magazine,' 1831, 'On some of the Characteristics of Modern Poetry and on the Lyrical Poems of ALFRED TENNYSON.' With an Introductory Note by RICHARD LE GALLIENNE. Small 8vo, 5s. net.

DE GRUCHY (AUGUSTA) UNDER THE HAWTHORN, AND OTHER VERSES. With Frontispiece by WALTER CRANE. Crown 8vo, 5s. net.

Also 30 copies on Japanese vellum, 15s. net.

GRAY (JOHN) SILVERPOINTS (POEMS). Printed in Italics. With Ornaments by C. S. RICKETTS. Long 12mo, 7s. 6d. net. [*All sold.*

Also 25 copies L. P., on hand-made paper. Bound in English vellum, £1, 1s. net. [*All sold.*

VAN DYKE (HENRY) THE POETRY OF TENNYSON. Third Edition, enlarged and revised. Crown 8vo, 5s. 6d. net.

The additions consist of a portrait, two extra chapters, and the Chronology expanded. The Laureate himself gave valuable aid in the correction of various details.

IMAGE (SELWYN) POEMS. With decorations by HERBERT PERCY HORNE. 12mo, 5s. net. [*In preparation.*

DE TABLEY (LORD) POEMS DRAMATIC AND LYRICAL. By JOHN LEICESTER WARREN, LORD DE TABLEY, M.A., F.S.A. With 5 Illustrations, and Cover (petals) designed by C. S. RICKETTS, and Book-plate by W. BELL SCOTT. Second Edition. Crown 8vo, 7s. 6d. net.

JOHNSON (LIONEL) THE ART OF THOMAS HARDY: SIX ESSAYS. With Etched Portrait from Life by WILLIAM STRANG, and a Bibliography by JOHN LANE. Crown 8vo, 5s. 6d. net.

Also a limited number on Large Paper, £1, 1s. net.

JOHNSON (LIONEL) POEMS. Fcap. 8vo, 5s. net.

[*In preparation.*

MEYNELL (MRS.) THE RHYTHM OF LIFE, AND OTHER ESSAYS. Second Edition. Fcap. 8vo, 3s. 6d. net.

Also 50 copies L. P., on hand-made paper, 12s. 6d. net.

MEYNELL (MRS.) POEMS. Second Edition. Fcap. 8vo, 3s. 6d. net.

Also 50 copies L. P., on hand-made paper, 12s. 6d. net.

WICKSTEED (P. H.) DANTE: SIX SERMONS. Third Edition, much improved. Crown 8vo, 2s. net.

FIELD (MICHAEL) STEPHANIA: A TRIALOGUE, IN THREE ACTS. Frontispiece, Colophon, and Ornament for binding designed by SELWYN IMAGE. Pott 4to, 6s. net.

FIELD (MICHAEL) SIGHT AND SONG. (Poems on Pictures.) 12mo, 5s. net. (Very few remain.)

HAMILTON (COL. IAN, V.C.) THE BALLAD OF HADJI, AND OTHER POEMS. Etched Frontispiece by WILLIAM STRANG. 12mo, 3s. net.

A FELLOWSHIP IN SONG. (POEMS.) By RICHARD LE GALLIENNE, NORMAN GALE, and ALFRED HAYES. Printed at the Rugby Press on hand-made paper, Small 8vo, 300 copies, 10s. 6d. net. [*All sold.*

Also 50 Large Paper, £1, 10s. net. [*All sold.*

BENSON (ARTHUR CHRISTOPHER) POEMS. 5s. net.

GREENE (G. A.) ITALIAN LYRISTS OF TO-DAY, Translations in the original metres from the Italian of CARDUCCI, STECCHETTI, D'ANNUNZIO, PANZACCHI, FOGAZZARO, GRAF, and about twenty other living writers, with bibliographical and biographical notes, and an introduction. 5s. net.

www.ingramcontent.com/pod-product-compliance
Lightning Source LLC
Chambersburg PA
CBHW030844270326
41928CB00007B/1208
* 9 7 8 3 7 4 4 7 6 7 5 5 2 *